GLENN McCRACKEN
NEW CASTLE AREA SCHOOLS
NEW CASTLE, PENNSYLVANIA

CHARLES C. WALCUTT
QUEENS COLLEGE
FLUSHING, NEW YORK

in collaboration with

MARY F. BOND
STATE COLLEGE AT FRAMINGHAM
FRAMINGHAM, MASSACHUSETTS

ESTHER FAIRCLOTH
MALDEN PUBLIC SCHOOLS
MALDEN, MASSACHUSETTS

B BOOK

TEACHER'S EDITION

LIPPINCOTT'S BASIC READING

J. B. LIPPINCOTT COMPANY
PHILADELPHIA
NEW YORK

ISBN-0-397-43309-3

Printed in the United States of America

10.7210.7

Contents

A MESSAGE TO THE TEACHER FROM THE AUTHORS

What Is Reading?

At first glance, it would hardly seem worth the trouble to answer this question because, in a sense, everybody knows perfectly well what reading is. But definitions underline all intellectual enterprises, and since definitions are also assumptions, they control the activities that are based on them. Another way of saying this is that "definitions are programs": they establish the terms in which people will think about an undertaking. Until modern times, medical knowledge was controlled by the assumption that there were four "humours" (blood, phlegm, yellow bile, and black bile) which determined a person's health and temperament. With these assumptions, it was impossible for a doctor to "see" many facts that remained invisible because the theory of humours did not permit them to exist.

Our definition of reading here is an attempt to explain the theory and practice upon which BASIC READING rests. To define reading, we must try to get at the element that sets it apart from other similar activities. It will not do, for example, to define reading as a thought-getting process, because we get thoughts just as surely from a lecture or a conversation. There is, to put it another way, no difference between "reading" a page of difficult philosophy and trying to understand it—and simply hearing the same page "read" to us by another. The problem of understanding is virtually identical for both reader and listener. So to call reading a thought-getting activity is not to identify what is particular to it.

Of course nobody would deny that the purpose of reading is to get information of some sort from the printed page. But since we get information in the same way from spoken language, this purpose does not define reading in a way that distinguishes it from talking. As soon as we grasp this point, however, the problem becomes somewhat simpler. If we see that meaning resides in language, then we can ask how writing (which we read) is related to language (which we hear and say). If language, which is sound, carries the meanings, what is writing? It seems obvious that writing is a device, a *code* if you like, for representing the sounds of language by visual forms. The written words are in fact visual symbols of the spoken words, which are sounds.

We have said that definitions, being assumptions, control the activities that are based on them. The literature on reading contains a tremendous amount of discussion on this question of the definition of itself. The richness and variety of this discussion springs from the fact that the whole field of reading theory and practice has been in a healthy state of experiment and change for many years. The debate over the definition of reading reflects this vitality.

It seems, therefore, appropriate to offer here a comprehensive definition that will not only guide and satisfy those who are using these textbooks, but will also show where our undertaking stands in relation to the whole picture of reading theory and practice today.

The problem of definition derives from the fact that the word reading has a good many meanings, several of which are involved when we speak of reading instruction in the primary grades.* The word means *pronounce, interpret, hear, search, apprehend, say aloud, study, discover the true nature of, assume a meaning, learn, gain information, have a specific wording,* and *have a certain quality*—and this list is far from exhaustive!

We propose that reading, as we commonly use the word in connection with teaching children, beginning at about age six, has three meanings simultaneously. These meanings do not exclude one another, but rather must be seen as coexisting in the word if we are to enjoy a satisfying and productive use of it. We will identify these meanings as *reading*[1], *reading*[2], and *reading*[3], as the linguists and semanticists use these indices. Let us consider them in the order in which they grow, but always with the understanding that no one of them explains what we are doing when we teach a child to read.

The surprising and interesting thing is how different the three meanings are.

Reading[1] is decoding the printed visual symbols into spoken sounds, which they designate. Reading, in other words, is turning writing into language. Language, as all the linguistics experts assure us, is spoken sound. Writing is a visual symbolization of those sounds, just as a musical score is a visual representation of the sounds of music. Reading converts writing into language, just as a pianist converts a score into music. It is symbol into sound in both instances, the former made with the mouth and vocal apparatus, the latter with fingers on a keyboard. This definition holds whether or not the spoken sound is understood, and it holds at both ends of a great scale. For example, at one end we can read a passage from a difficult poem without understanding it. At the other ends of this scale, a child can read a single word like *fid* without understanding it. In both cases, we are converting printed symbols into proper sounds. We are turning writing into language. The parallel with music holds here too. A person might tap out the notes of a complex sonata without either grasping or reproducing the meaning of the piece; yet hitting the right notes is the first and essential step toward rendering and interpreting the musical score.

Reading[2] is, strangely enough, not really reading at all! It is *understanding language,* yet it is the goal that we demand immediately upon the mastery of *reading*[1]. The distinction may be clarified with an illustration. Suppose we read aloud to you the most difficult of Shakespeare's sonnets. Suppose, for the sake of our argument, that you do not understand it.

* What follows reproduces the essence of "Reading—a Professional Definition," by Charles C. Walcutt, printed in THE ELEMENTARY SCHOOL JOURNAL, April, 1967.

Is anything the matter with your reading? Obviously not, for you are not reading, but listening. Your problem is a problem of understanding language. But now, and more important, suppose that we who have read the sonnet to you do not understand it either. Would you say that anything was the matter with our reading? You might, but on reflection you would have to admit that our difficulty was exactly the same as yours—a difficulty with the language. You certainly would not send us to a remedial reading teacher, but to an expert on Shakespeare. So what we call reading here is actually *understanding language*. It is *reading*[2]. We certainly have it in mind when we speak of reading. It is the element of communication that is the goal of any reading instruction, but it is the same process that applies in spoken discourse and communication.

Reading[3] is hardest to define, but essential to our use of the word. On a higher level, reading takes us into a world of art and intellect that is accessible only through the printed page. Whether history, anthropology, poetry, fiction, or philosophy is involved, we move into worlds of written discourse that are not accessible, and indeed do not exist, in spoken language. The literary style that is an essential form of the highest human thought depends on writing. We do not find the same style, the same quality of language, the same discrimination and breadth of vocabulary in spoken discourse. Where these higher qualities have appeared in spoken discourse, they have appeared there as a consequence of having been developed in writing. The intricate form of a sonnet or a Spenserian stanza, the elaborate form of a sentence by Macaulay or Gibbon, the close structure of an essay by John Stuart Mill (a hundred other examples would do as well) have all been developed through the written language, which permits the kind of study, elaboration, and accuracy that probably could not be sustained with only a spoken language.

It is true that the epic and the ballad seem to have been developed orally. They were composed, performed, and transmitted by professional minstrels, it appears, and constitute special cases. During most periods of the historical past, it has been a commonplace that access to learning—which meant writing—brought special privileges of culture and power. The House of Intellect, which is the accumulated culture of man—which in other words is the Mind of the past brought up to and poured into the Mind of the present—has been both wrought and stored in the written word. The realms of gold, the hoardings of the world's great books, exist only in books and by virtue of the art of writing. *Reading*[3] takes us into these realms of gold, which are the reward of reading.

The first steps into *reading*[3] come as early as the child begins to read a language that he does not hear spoken. As early as third grade, surely, and often in the second the child who has learned to read will be coming upon hundreds of words that he does not say or hear, words that become part of his reading vocabulary—and these are found in sentences of a style and a precision that he will rarely hear spoken. Together, the rich precise literary vocabulary and the sentences and paragraphs of skilled writing carry a level of art and thought that rises above—though it rests upon—the very summit of spoken discourse.

The specialists in linguistics emphasize the fact that language is spoken sound and that a particular language is to be known through its spoken patterns. These are what linguistic anthropologists record with special symbols in the remotest villages, say, of Africa. It is the spoken language, furthermore, that finally seems to determine usage: a language grows in speech. We accept these considerations, but we also affirm that there are, indeed, two languages—the spoken language and the written language—and that we learn to read in order to read the written language.

There is no particular value to having first- or second-grade readers in the spoken language—that is, using only the vocabulary and the sentence structures that a first- or second-grade child would *himself* use. Reading takes the child into a different world, and this world is different precisely because it is the magical world of the written language.

And now another point that this definition clarifies: reading instruction that begins with a sight vocabulary skips over *reading*[1] and goes on to *reading*[2], with the special complication that it attaches meaning directly to the printed symbol. Such instruction treats printing, that is, as if it were language. A sight word is taught first as a meaning rather than as a symbol of a sound. Using context and picture clues, the child is led to reason and guess what a word may mean, rather than to figure out what sound that printed word represents and then go on to refer the sound to his knowledge of language. Under this approach, reading is defined as "bringing meaning to the printed page," and the definition clearly reveals that the child is being led to *deduce* the meaning of a printed word in a sentence rather than to *decode* that printed word into its proper sound and then *understand the language* that he has unlocked.

Parallels with music flood over us at this point. The virtuoso pianist pours out his interpretation without any thought about individual notes or scales, yet he had to learn those notes and scales with painstaking repetition and practice before he could be liberated from them. So with reading. The more carefully and accurately the mechanical skill of decoding the print into sound is mastered, the sooner it can be forgotten in the delight of accurate reading for meaning and enjoyment. Fortunately, the skill of reading is a great deal easier to learn than playing the piano!

Theory and Practice

Now, what is the value of our definition as regards the teaching of reading? We believe its value is that it enables us to put first things first and approach the task of learning to read, with our children, in an orderly and effective manner. We are intensely concerned that our children understand what they read, but the "decoding" skill must come first if we are to get them started properly.

For the truth is that the language, the imagination, the experience, and the conversation of a typical six-year-old child are enormously far beyond anything he is going to be able to read for some time. It will be quite a few months before anything he can read will even approach the vocabulary and thought of what he has heard or even spoken himself. We believe this is more true today than it was in the past. What the child hears on radio or television is often very advanced linguistically compared to what he will read in his first books.

So the faster we teach him the skill, the faster will his ability to read catch up with his language, which, of course, has had a six-year head-start. Once he has mastered the skill, this relation changes radically: *reading*[3] becomes the prime source of growth in vocabulary, in language, and in intellect. Within a very few years the child who has learned to read properly will be reading and understanding hundreds and hundreds of words that he may not regularly speak or hear until he is attending lectures in college!

In view of these facts, we do not hesitate to say that the rewards of the first steps in reading are not impressive growth in experience or vocabulary. There are rewards, however, of two sorts. First, there is the great satisfaction of mastering a skill in an orderly fashion. If an analogy will help here, we might say that first steps in reading are like first steps in learning to drive an automobile. Both skills have enormous attractions to the young learner, for they are gateways to many joys. The learning car-driver has these rewards in mind, but at the start he is totally engrossed simply in the activity of learning to drive. At this stage he has no thought of going anywhere; learning to operate the automobile is reward and interest enough in itself. And so it is with reading. The reward of emulating the grownups, for whom reading is obviously very important, is the long-range goal; but the skill itself is reward and delight for the beginner.

On top of this delight in learning for itself, we seek to reward the young learner with amusing or exciting stories as fast as we have the words for them; and in fact we accumulate vocabulary very much more rapidly than has been done with the standard basal readers in recent years. Yet, even though this program accumulates a vocabulary well in excess of 2,000 words in the first grade (as contrasted with as few as 325 words in standard basal readers) and proceeds in a similar fashion in subsequent grades, the teacher will be surprised to discover how very elementary it is and how very far beneath the actual speaking and hearing vocabularies of her pupils it is.

The pleasure and confidence of the child are reinforced by the outstanding feature of this program: With the exception of a handful of special words, every story contains only the letter-sounds that have been taught at any point. No letter or spelling appears until after the lesson in which it is presented.

Some Linguistic Aspects of Reading

At this point we should like to make it clear that BASIC READING offers more than many of the new so-called linguistic systems of reading instruction. It uses various principles that have been strongly and properly emphasized by the linguistics specialists. But it also incorporates many of the best characteristics of the standard basal systems; and it has an entirely new system of presenting letters, sound-spellings, words, and sentences in a *coherent* and *integrated* pattern. This latter, as we shall explain, is what sets it apart from other reading programs.

On the question of beginning instruction with *reading*[1], however, we are in total accord with the best linguistic thinking, which declares that "language is spoken sound" and that reading instruction must first establish the relations between the spoken sounds and the letters that spell them. As you know, this position has been challenged since the early 1920's by those who believe that reading should begin with experience charts, paragraphs, sentences, and whole words. The argument against beginning with sounds and letters is too complex for us to answer in full. We should, rather, prefer to dispose of it as simply as possible. Let us just touch on what may seem to be the strongest point—that much English spelling is so irregular, so "un-phonic," that it defies a systematic approach. But we begin with the most regular spellings, the short vowels and the sounded consonants, and with these alone we accumulate vocabulary very quickly and use it in meaningful sentences and stories. We do not stress spelling patterns to the point of monotony or absurdity. Let us illustrate with three examples: In "Oh! oh! Look, look, something!" we have very common words with very irregular, un-simple spellings. In "Pat can bat at a fat cat," we have highly consistent spelling patterns without much sense in the sentence. In our system you may find a sentence like "Dan bent his dad's fender," which is made of three short vowels and only eight sounded consonants—and makes sense as a sentence. Here, then, we combine the virtues of basal readers and linguistic principles without the shortcomings of either.

Now, to return to the argument against beginning with sounds and letters, we offer what may at first glance seem to be a startling contradiction: We contend that the irregular spelling of so many common words constitutes the strongest argument for beginning with the regular elements of English spelling. Why? Simply because if our spelling system is approximately 85 per cent regular, it would seem proper to begin with the regular system before taking up the exceptions. This is the heart of our method. We find that when the child learns, at the beginning, one consistent thing after another, he rapidly gains understanding and confidence. There are no mysterious configurations that he must memorize without clues, so that he may confuse words like *after* and *alter,* or even little words like *then* and *always.* Rather, he learns why and how the letters represent the sounds of the word. With this clue, his learning is vastly simplified and accelerated. Our aim is to make him recognize words instantly, and we find that he does this with the least drill when he knows why the letters that make up a certain word are there. If we give him a dozen sight words, he may confuse *then* and *always* because he knows them only as pure configurations; but when he knows the letters first, he understands why these letters spell the sound of the word, and his recognition of the *whole word* at a glance (which is the goal of *any* reading system) is easier for him than it would have been if he had learned the same word only as a whole, without benefit of the previous training in letters.

At this point we should like to refine our definition of *reading*[1] with a further thought. If learning language is learning the meanings of sounds (i.e., words), learning *reading*[1] is *learning letter significance,* for the entire system of alphabetic writing is based on the use of letters to indicate individual sounds. The phoneme-grapheme (i.e. sound-spelling) relations in English orthography seem very imperfect when we look at strange spelling like *might, cough, should, colonel, sleigh,* and *machine.* And indeed English orthography is needlessly bad, for we use 26 letters to spell 44 basic phonemes in more than 250 different ways. That is one side of the matter; but if we look at all the words that are spelled regularly, and then set about organizing the irregular spellings into minor groups and patterns, we find that it is not an impossible accomplishment. And if we begin with the regular system, it is not at all difficult to master the exceptions when they are taken up, later, one group at a time.

Sound and Sense: Basic Letter Knowledge with No "Sounding Out"

Many teachers wonder whether the mechanical process of "sounding out" a strange word will not interfere with a child's ability to attend to its meaning. They know that a child may have trouble putting two isolated sounds together, and they fear that the struggle to do so may drive all thought of meaning out of his mind. This could be a real problem. A child may have the greatest difficulty looking at letters individually and then trying to say-them-together into a syllable or word. We have solved this problem by virtually eliminating the laborious pronouncing and combining of isolated sounds.

Impossible?

Not at all. Indeed, very simple. It is merely a question of method.

Let us begin with the solid assumption that the child hears and says thousands of words just about as well as we do. So he knows the sounds-combined that are words. Our task is to help him hear the phonemes in the words that he hears and says very well. He says "fat" perfectly. Beginning there, we get him to recognize, to identify its three sounds. At the same time we show him how the three letters represent these sounds. This can all be done without any sounding-out at all: we begin with the whole word, identify its phonemes, and then connect those sounds with their spellings.

As you will see in the detailed instructions in this manual, we first demonstrate to the child how the two letter-sounds of *a* and *m* are brought together to make the word *am.* Thereafter, with every letter presented we make new words; but instead of asking the child to grasp the letters together as a word, we consistently show him how the phoneme-grapheme relationships appear in the new words. This is effectively done through demonstration by the teacher. Having taught *a, n,* and then *r,* we demonstrate *r-a-n . . . ran* by showing how the sounds occur in the word. To put it another way, we teach the words and wholes while we lead the child to see how the sounds that he knows occur in each word and are systematically represented by the letters in it.

With these principles in mind, we are confident that you will see that it is very important not to strive for ultimate mastery in sound recognition for the first five lessons, which present the five short vowels. To try to teach complete mastery of these vowels in isolation is to violate the principles we have been setting forth. These lessons are intended 1.) to provide simplified readiness materials; 2.) to acquaint children with the idea of a printed letter, that is, its existence and appearance; and 3.) to show them that a letter represents a sound. Remember that every single word in the book has a vowel in it! You begin to teach reading on the sixth page when two letter-sounds are brought together in a word.

Rather than to linger over the first five lessons, experienced and successful teachers hasten to the sixth lesson so that they can move more slowly from there on. There is no question that the first steps in reading words must be taken slowly. As soon as the children have grasped the elements involved—that is, the meaning of letters—they will go ahead at increasing speeds. Once they are well started, able children may gobble up several new letters and sounds in a day.

We have been asked why we begin with vowels instead of consonants, and what is the significance of the order of our consonants and sound-spellings? Before answering these questions, we should like to make some preliminary observations. We have found that to a six-year-old beginning reader the technical and theoretical difference between a vowel and a consonant is both irrelevant and unimportant! You might be able to explain it to him, but he would surely forget it soon, *if* he ever understood you. We don't believe that one adult in a hundred can explain what a vowel is, although he can memorize and recite their names as well as any child can.

Nor is there any *significant* difference to a child between hearing two consonants in a blend and hearing a vowel-consonant combination that makes a syllable or a word. It is easier to *say* the syllable, of course, but we are interested at first in teaching the child to hear or recognize how two sounds are combined. This is done with the inner ear, rather than said. So far as hearing goes, there is no essential difference to a child between the two phonemes in the sound that we write *sm* and the two phonemes that we write *so;* he hears one combination as easily as the other. But in the first stages it is an advantage for him to be able to say while he hears; so we let him begin with words rather than with blends. He learns the blends easily as soon as he comes to them in words, a few lessons later.

Why did we use the letter-order we have? First, we begin with the short vowels because they appear in every word (except the occasional *y*-word, but they come in much later), and we present them without teaching them as isolated sounds. These short vowels also permit the construction of short words free from such complexities as digraphs and the silent or signal *e* of such words as *late*. Then we go to consonants because, of course, you have to add them to vowels to make words. The particular consonants were chosen for two important reasons: 1) We naturally begin with high-frequency consonants because having them enables us to make the most two-, three-, and four-letter words easily. If, at the other extreme, we had begun with *q, x, y*, and *z*, we could not have made many simple words! 2) Equally important is the fact that our first consonants, *m, n, r,* and *s* are *continuants* rather than *plosives*. Their sounds can be sustained indefinitely, just like a vowel sound. One can draw out *m-m-m-m* or *s-s-s-s* as long as his breath lasts. Plosives, like *b, t,* or *p* demand a sudden opening of the breathstream and so cannot be sustained. For the first steps in reading the difference is important. Now, notice the ease with which the sounds of *aaaaaaa-mmmmmm* can be run together orally, or *mmmmm-aaaa-nnnn*. The opening of the lips at the end of the *mmmm* sound leads naturally to the *a* sound. The *r* in *ran* is said with the lips apart and flows naturally into the *a*.

At first, when we are demonstrating how the sounds go together, the continuants are much easier to manage. After four of them, the secret will have been grasped, and we go on to the plosives, *t* and *d*. While we are on the point, we should like to stress the fact that the *essence of reading* can be learned with the vowels and those first four consonants. So *here* is where to take your time and get a solid start.

Thus we begin with simple spellings in simple, familiar words. All the sounds are on the whole equally easy for a typical child; he knows them all and has known them for years. We want to begin with simple words that are simply *spelled*. Instead of vocabulary control in terms of word frequency, we use phoneme-grapheme (i.e. sound-spelling) control in terms of simplicity and regularity—moving into the irregular spellings after the regular ones have been mastered.

You will see, as you work with the system, that the steady accumulation of new words, first in lists and then in stories (which, let us emphasize again, use only the letter-sounds that have been taught up to any point), comes as the child learns to recognize letter-sounds in words. He gets the word as a whole while he recognizes the letter elements that spell it on the page.

This procedure not only avoids the dangers inherent in labored sounding out, but also from the very beginning teaches the children to see words as wholes. The whole sound-spelling patterns and the whole meaning patterns are joined into a single unit of perception. This is another way of saying that we want every word the child learns to become a "sight" word for him, in the sense that he recognizes it instantly as a whole. This goal is tremendously simplified and expedited if the child, while seeing the word as a whole, also knows the letters that make it and knows why those particular letters make it. He need not pronounce the word either aloud or to himself, but he recognizes the printed word as a systematic representation of the spoken word—because he knows the system.

In short, following this program the child learns from the beginning to see words exactly as the most skillful adult readers see them: not as configurations or silhouettes, but as whole images of complete words with all their letters. We have these images—of thousands and thousands of words—already in our minds, and it is these perfect images of the whole words that we see as we read rapidly. So remarkable is the trigger-mechanism of the brain that a good reader, going at top speed, will actually see *answer* when the word on the page is misprinted as *ansmer*. What clues the human perceptive apparatus uses in perceiving words so rapidly is still a mystery.

We should like to take this occasion to clear up a myth about reading that recurs with surprising frequency. It is that the people who believe in a phonic-linguistic approach teach what is termed "word calling" and do not care about "reading for meaning." If we stress sound-spelling relationships, it is precisely because we are deeply concerned to cut the most direct and reliable path to meaning. As we have said earlier, printing is a visual means of representing the sounds which are language. Meaning is in these sounds. We want to equip the child to turn the written word into a spoken word (whether he actually utters it or not) so he will hear what it says, that is, get its meaning. If a child looks at a picture or thinks about the context—and then says "dish" when the printed word is "bowl," he is not reading for meaning: he is guessing. And guessing is not good enough.

Furthermore, in all our experience we have never found anybody who did not think that the purpose of reading was to get the meaning. The only possible defense of skipping sound and going directly from print to meaning would be that printed words are directly meaningful—that the printed word *green* means the color, but this is not so. It is the spoken word *green* that designates the color, while the printed word designates the sound of the spoken word. Various linguistics specialists have recently been stressing this fact.

Some of the Less Obvious Aspects of Our Phonic-Linguistic System

People continually ask questions about the phonic-linguistic system of BASIC READING—questions which reveal that many teachers would like to know about some of the planning that went into its formulation. By phonetics we mean precisely the *sounds* of the English language. These sounds existed for thousands of years before there was any writing or spelling. When the system of writing with an alphabet was invented (and this was long before the English language had evolved from its distant Indo-European roots), it could only have made possible an approximate representation of the enormous variety of speech sounds in any language.

We can illustrate this point by jumping ahead into a current example: the sound represented by the spelling *to* varies from the complete pronunciation that one might give if dictating the word for a spelling lesson, to the barest and almost inaudible *t* that we sense rather than hear when one says rapidly, "I'm going down to the store before it closes."

Or consider the word "the" as it might be dictated for a spelling lesson, ending in a clear long *e*, against the same word in the middle of a sentence, where it comes out as a barely-heard *th*.

Thousands of such variations in speech sounds have never been represented by any alphabetic spelling, in whatever language. Now if we consider the fact that our alphabet was invented for an earlier and different language from English, plus the fact that both the sounds and the spellings of English have evolved enormously during the past thousand years, plus the further fact that these two—the evolution of English sounds and the evolution of English spelling—have not by any means been consistently geared to each other, we can understand that our spelling renders only an approximation of our language sounds. But perhaps more surprising, on first thought, is the fact that this inaccuracy, this approximateness, is tremendously valuable. It is what makes writing possible! A Maine Yankee and a Southerner from deepest Georgia can both read a novel written in eighteenth-century England by someone who pronounced the language very differently from either of them. If the spelling represented the sounds more exactly, this would not be possible. The Maine Yankee can write a letter to his cousin in Georgia, furthermore, and be easily understood precisely *because* his spelling only approximately indicates his speech sounds. A moment's reflection tells us that we all, without even thinking about it, make the adjustment between the way a sentence is spelled out in writing and the way we ourselves say it.

Children learning to read are constantly making the same sorts of adjustments, which they make with very little instruction. They have been speaking for years before they began reading, and speech was as "natural" to them as walking. Because speech is "natural," we do not even think about a great many of the sounds that we hear and pronounce. If you ask twenty people at random whether they know that the initial sounds of *th*in and *th*en are different sounds, most of them will tell you that they never thought of it. We spell the two different sounds *th* and adjust to the correct pronunciation—most of us—without realizing that there are two different sounds! Now for an amusing variation, let us consider the fact that the difference between initial *th* in *thin* and *then* is *exactly* the same kind of difference as that between the initial sounds of *fin* and *van*—which we spell with different letters. The first is "unvoiced," the second "voiced," which is all the difference. Probably not more than one person in fifty is aware of this fact—or of the same relation between *p* and *b* and between *s* and *z* and between *k* and *g*. In some cases we spell the sounds with different letters, and in some cases with the same letters. This is a complex and inconsistent procedure, but we get along very well with it; and indeed we get along very well, most of us, totally ignorant of the existence of such intricacies.

Our point is that the child learning to read is dealing with a system of writing that only approximates an accurate representation of the sounds. The child's guide and resource is his own speaking and hearing knowledge of the language. He identifies the written word, an imperfect symbol, with his own long and deeply established speaking knowledge of that word. He connects the *s* in *saw* with its sound, and then he connects the *s* in *was* with its different sound (it's a *z* in *was,* of course)—and the words come so naturally to him that he may not even realize that different sounds are represented by the *s*.

This explains why, relying on the child's own language knowledge, we have in BASIC READING not emphasized many phonetic complexities that the child does not have to be bothered with while he is learning to read. If he says varying sounds so naturally that he is unaware of their difference, so much the better for him! A trained linguist can explain that the *a* of *came* is a different sound from the *a* of *care*. We present the two words in nearby lessons without any notice of the difference, because the child does not need to be bothered with it. Few people have noticed that the *n* in *band* represents a very different sound from the *n* in *bank*. We present the *nd* in *Book A* and *nk* in *Book B,* but the latter is deferred only because the *k* comes in *Book B* in our sound-spelling sequence. No attention at all need be given to the fact that these are different *n* sounds, because every child says and hears them correctly. The *n* in *bank* is the same sound that is spelled *ng* in *sing,* which comes in *Book C,* but of course no special notice need be made of this fact.

Thus, what may seem to be oversights in BASIC READING are in fact carefully planned simplifications that make it easier for the child to learn to read. The professional linguistics scholar may delight in explaining the difference between the *a* in *came* and the *a* in *care*—but no child should be unduly concerned with it. It is more of a problem for college-level phonetics or linguistics.

Some Special Aspects of the Program

Readiness

A special aspect of this program is the "Accompanying Readiness," or "Functional Readiness," which teaches the readiness skills at the same time that the child is learning the names, and shapes, of the first letters. This new approach to readiness is a tremendous time-saver. The pupil actually learns to read in the few weeks formerly devoted entirely to readiness. The teacher using this manual will see how naturally the two experiences go together. There is also an advantage in flexibility: the readiness exercises may be omitted whenever they are no longer needed.

Eighteen of the usual readiness skills developed at the first-grade level are "built in" the first eleven pages of *Book A*. Skills suggested in the lesson plans for these pages are:

1. Recognition of colors
2. Left-to-right eye movement
3. Recognition of similarities and differences
4. Relationships
5. Concepts of *more, less,* and *fewer*
6. Following sequence of events to tell a story
7. Awareness of page numbers

8. Counting
9. Recognition of position relationships
10. Oral expression
11. Recalling details to relate a story
12. Awareness of differences in shapes
13. Line-to-line sequence
14. Interpretation of a picture story
15. Making inferences
16. Understanding of ordinals (1-6)
17. Auditory discrimination
18. Association and recognition of upper and lower case letters

The Teacher's Edition presents a suggested procedure for developing the readiness skills with the class, and there are pages in the *Book A* Workbook that serve the same end.

Special Words

Since our aim is to build the largest possible vocabulary of instantly recognized "sight" words, we use the term *special* to designate the handful of words that we have had to present, in order to be able to write stories, before their linguistic elements have been taught. In *Book A* these words are *a, the, to, put,* and *for.* They are usually presented as slight variants from the pattern of the lesson in which they appear, and there are so few of them that they will never interfere with the child's mastery of the consistent basic system of sound-spellings.

Book B contains ten *special* words, and *Book C* contains eleven. There are no *special* words in *Book D.*

Consideration for Learners of Varying Abilities

It has been said of most basic reading programs that the material presented was either too much of a load for the slower learner or not challenging enough for the child blessed with exceptional ability. This program has been designed with children of various abilities in mind. In teaching the 44 sounds and presenting more than 2,000 words at the Grade One level, we present adequate material to keep the bright pupil well occupied. But the slower learning pupil need not study and master every one of the words that appear in the word lists because not all these words are necessary for successful reading of the accompanying stories. The pupils work with the word lists until they become familiar with the phoneme-grapheme relationships involved and can recognize them in new or unfamiliar words.

Book E, the first level of the Grade Two program, reviews in the same sequence, but in larger units, all the sound-spellings developed in the Grade One program. A pupil who has not completed all of *Book D* of the Grade One program need not, therefore, go back to complete it; but he can begin *Book E,* proceeding at a comfortable pace.

Workbooks, duplicating masters, and textfilms, all of which will be discussed later, provide additional tools for working with pupils of varying abilities.

The Use of the Workbook

Workbooks, properly used, can become a valuable part of a complete developmental reading program. The activities in the BASIC READING Workbooks are designed to be done in the time allotted for reading instruction. They are not designed merely to keep the child occupied while the teacher does something else. Each exercise reinforces or develops an essential reading skill.

The workbook should be the culminating activity for each lesson. This does not mean that there must be a workbook exercise every day. At the bottom of every workbook page is a note to the teacher explaining the purpose of the page and telling what lesson in the text it follows. The Teacher's Editions for the student textbooks also contain similar instructions for correlation.

Beginning with the *Book C* Workbook, directions for use appear at the top of each page. They are placed there so that the teacher can ask her group to read them silently before calling on a single child to read them aloud and then discussing the procedures involved until they are understood by everyone. A child working on an exercise he does not understand is, of course, wasting his time. Most teachers find it desirable to do the first part of an exercise with the group, before leaving them to work by themselves. The workbooks serve the triple function of teaching, practice, and review. The more carefully an exercise is launched, with explanation and demonstration, the more it will accomplish for the child.

After they have finished an exercise, children enjoy reading some of their answers aloud. The teacher may add to this "refreshment" by sending a pupil or two to the chalkboard to write some of the important words they have been learning.

After this, it is desirable to check the workbook lessons immediately—and best of all, we think, to have each pupil correct his answers before the teacher collects the workbooks for her own examination of them.

The Use of Duplicating Masters

Duplicating masters, also properly used, can serve as a valuable adjunct to an effective reading program. A box of duplicating masters has been prepared for each of the books in the primary (Grades One-Three) program. In certain cases, these duplicating masters duplicate teaching suggestions in the Teacher's Editions, freeing the teacher from the time-consuming process of creating her own masters for reproduction. The general instructions for effective use of workbooks, previously mentioned, are appropriate for the duplicating masters.

The Use of the Textfilms

Textfilms were prepared especially to accompany and augment the BASIC READING series. Throughout the three primary-grade levels, there is at least one filmstrip frame to accompany each lesson in the program. The teacher will thus have carefully-correlated projected images to improve the teaching of every reading skill during the entire school year.

In most instances the filmstrip frames teach the same lessons as those they accompany in the textbooks, except that the film lessons are greatly condensed. This plan affords the teacher opportunities to use the film frames for introducing lessons and clarifying meanings before transferring to the textbook lessons, where she may extend the teaching and test the learning.

Careful classroom testing over a period of several years has proved this type of textfilm to be effective for various reasons:

1. For motivation of pupil interest, film can seldom be surpassed as an effective teaching tool. Attention spans are greatly lengthened. It is not unusual for a Grade-One teacher to hold the undivided attention of an entire class for as long as forty minutes while teacher and pupils work at a screen on just one image. Interest is a basic prerequisite to reading success. These textfilms will stimulate pupils' interest and curiosity so that the teacher will enjoy an ideal learning situation.
2. The textfilm provides an excellent medium for introducing new material vividly and clearly so that children can understand meanings and follow directions.
3. These textfilms provide a useful and convenient method for reviewing and testing material already taught in the textbook lessons. They are particularly helpful for this purpose because the material is greatly condensed in the films. Reviewing and testing of various lessons may be accomplished in less time than would otherwise be required.
4. The film image is large and colorful, and it appears at the front of the classroom where it is readily viewed by every pupil. All the children in the room may participate in each lesson.
5. Class management is thus simplified while textfilm frames are being projected because the children are all attentive to what is going on at the screen.
6. Film complements and reinforces other teaching techniques. It is a vivid, stimulating, clarifying, and concrete approach. This is the type of lesson presentation that has proved most successful with the slower-learner.

A decision you will be making as you plan to teach reading with the BASIC READING series with textfilms is whether you will group your children into ability sections for initial lesson instruction. Many teachers choose the whole-class approach in which each new lesson is presented to the entire class at the same time. Excellent results may be achieved with this latter method. In whole-class presentations the projection screen should be mounted over a section of the chalkboard at the front of the classroom. If, however, you prefer to separate your class into ability groups, then you may place the projection screen behind a piano or curtain so that only one section of the class may see it at a time. With small groups, darkening of the room is unnecessary.

Class Organization

Many factors will affect your decisions as to class organization. Local administrative practices and policies may be one factor; the abilities and competencies of the pupils is another; and whether or not homogeneous grouping is used is still another. Whole-class and small-group types of organization each have many advocates. BASIC READING has been designed to work equally well with either method of organization. Some teachers choose to begin the year with whole-group instruction, changing to small-group instruction as the year progresses and as the varying abilities of pupils come to light.

Communication and Creative Writing

One of the great improvements in the schools of our time springs from the discovery that children thrive on self-expression. A generation or so ago we saw the concept of self-expression as almost a cure-all that would make a child blossom, according to his own "needs" and nature, from encouragement and opportunity rather than direction and discipline. Every child was assumed to have an inherent growth pattern, along with an inherent capacity, that should not be tampered with or disturbed by imposed rigidities of program or instruction.

We have seen these views greatly modified during the past couple of decades, for we have discovered that an excess of permissiveness may be a damaging factor in a child's development. A later understanding finds that children need order, because order produces security, and nothing is more important for the child than security.

With these reservations, we wish, nevertheless, to urge that activities in creative writing that accompany this program be as free as possible. We believe that the children should from their first days in school be encouraged to express themselves by telling recent experiences, making up imaginative stories, and even composing rhymes. A feeling for language develops with its use. In a *setting* of order, restraint, and composure, the child may develop a feeling for communication, a feeling that he is expressing himself to a listening group.

Creative writing should follow the same patterns. That is, the occasion should be one of order and composure, but the writing itself should be free and uninhibited. We should not place undue emphasis upon handwriting or spelling, particularly the latter. Although BASIC READING begins with regular easy spellings, it is no secret that some of the commonest English words are irregularly spelled. If the child is to write freely, he must use these words that he does not know how to spell. It is best to let him spell them according to what letter knowledge he has at the moment, with the understanding that he will learn somewhat later how to spell them correctly. If the creative use of the language is praised, and the question of spelling subordinated as being a practical consideration that will be met later, the child will not be inhibited in trying to write a word that he has not learned how to spell.

The teacher may reward such free writing by having good stories read aloud to the class either by the pupil or by herself. Occasionally a good group of stories may be corrected by the teacher and returned for the pupils to take home. It is also stimulating if some of the best stories are correctly typed or printed and posted on the bulletin board or assembled in a class book. We do not recommend that the primitive, uncorrected papers be put on display for the other children to read. The more often a child is asked to correct and rewrite, at this level, the shorter and more stilted his future stories will become, so display only the ones that are correct at first. If we are affirmative and enthusiastic, we shall build a desire to write, and this is what we want most of all.

Regional Pronunciations

American English displays a very wide range of regional pronunciations—so wide that a Maine farmer and a Texas rancher may have some difficulty understanding each other, and perhaps even greater difficulty understanding speakers from certain areas of the deep South. Yet, as we have said earlier in this Message, these people read the same writing with equal ease. What this proves is that our alphabetic system of writing is an economical *approximation* of the sounds that it records. Wherever you teach, your pupils are going to speak in their local pronunciation and, generally, read in it. The question of refining students' speech toward a more "standard" English than they normally speak is not, strictly, a problem of reading instruction. Where localized pronunciations deviate from the examples in the textbooks, it is advisable to discuss briefly deviations in regional pronunciations while reassuring the pupils that their localized speech patterns are acceptable.

The Use of the Teacher's Editions

The Teacher's Editions for BASIC READING have been designed to present concisely complete suggestions for the development of effective teaching lessons. The suggestions provided are usually more than the teacher has time to use. Therefore, they should not be viewed as mandatory or prescriptive. Instead, the teacher, with intimate knowledge of the abilities of her class, will be able to draw from the suggestions those materials most suitable for her class or teaching group. The suggestions for enrichment, for additional stories and poems, films and filmstrips, and songs may all be used to help to provide for the individual differences in each class.

The suggested materials for the teacher are, for the most part, organized within a logical framework to provide for easy lesson planning. Following the description of the lesson or story with pages involved in the primary program, a section entitled Building Linguistic Skills or Introduction appears. In this section the phoneme-grapheme relationships are presented with pertinent teaching suggestions. Subsequently, sections on Procedure, Guiding Reading for Comprehension, Suggestions for Further Activities, and Enrichment occur. For ease of teacher reference, marginal annotations in a second color highlight the skills and objectives.

Materials in the Teacher's Editions are carefully balanced to provide for full utilization of multisensory approaches to learning. Exercises involving auditory discrimination are balanced with exercises involving visual discrimination so that close associations may be made. In addition, there appear exercises utilizing kinesthetic activities for further reinforcement. Suggestions for motivation, vocabulary building, word analysis, creative writing, correlations of auxiliary materials, guidance of silent and oral reading are readily and appropriately placed.

The Teacher's Editions for *Books F, G,* and *H,* contain a Linguistic Elements Guide which may be used effectively with those students who are in need of special help on certain linguistic elements. The teacher may find it helpful to use this Guide in remediation work with students who are, through absence, transfer, or otherwise, in need of special assistance. (*Note:* Permission to reproduce the Linguistic Elements Guide for classroom use is granted by the publisher.)

The Primary Program (Grades One, Two, and Three)

The First-Grade Program

The Grade One program of BASIC READING consists of four books, *Books A, B, C,* and *D.* These correspond in reading levels to Pre-Primer, Primer, 1-1 Reader, and 1-2 Reader respectively. It has already been stated that the fundamental strength of BASIC READING is in the synthetic development of word analysis skills. The lists of Basic Phonemes and Phoneme-Grapheme Relationships which appear at the end of the Grade One (*Books A, B, C, D*) readers illustrate the comprehensive manner in which major English sound-spellings are presented. Each lesson in the Grade One books presents a new linguistic element followed by poems or stories in which the linguistic element appears. Rigid control of the introduction of these linguistic elements is practiced. The pupil is therefore able to attack successfully new words containing previously taught linguistic elements. As the pupil progresses, he meets minor sound-spelling patterns and irregular sound-spellings. He also meets factors such as punctuation marks, sentence length, paragraphing, and story titles in carefully introduced order with full explanation at the time of introduction.

The Second-Grade Program

In *Book E* (first level of second reader) we review the phoneme-grapheme presentation of Grade One in exactly the same order, but instead of more than a hundred elements, taught in more than ninety lessons and stories, we have condensed the same materials into twelve Linguistic Units. Thus the stories rapidly become longer and more rewarding, as they should in a second-grade reader. If a class has mastered the system in Grade One, it can go through this reader rapidly; but wherever review or reteaching is necessary, you will find full treatment in this Teacher's Edition of any spelling—and many further exercises in the workbook. Linguistics Unit 12 introduces some new spellings, such as *guide, mountain,* and *whistle.*

In *Book F,* we may assume that the common English sound-spellings have been successfully presented, and so we proceed with an enriched vocabulary.

The stories and poems in *Book F* are grouped into six sections which reflect a certain unity of tone, style, or subject. The Teacher's Edition suggests a considerable variety of activities and projects that can make use of these groupings; but no teacher need be controlled by them if she wishes at any point in the term to relate her reading activities to some other aspect of the curriculum.

The Third-Grade Program

The stories and poems in the Third-Grade Readers (*Books G* and *H*) are presented in sections, the titles of which indicate the themes that unify them. As before, each Part in the Teacher's Edition opens with a general discussion of its contents; from this, the teacher can plan the extended activities toward which she will work. Suggestions for Correlated Activities come at the end of each section. The groupings need not prevent the teacher from taking stories up in an order that fits in with other studies in the curriculum.

For those teachers who desire to integrate the appreciation of literary values with language arts, activities involving composition, grammar, phonics, punctuation, and sentence structure are included in the Teacher's Edition.

BOOK B

Page 1 — Introduction of a followed by r

Building Linguistic Skills

phoneme-grapheme relationships

The combination of **a** and **r** and the resulting new vocabulary. Recognition of the word **are.**

Introduction

*introducing the **ar** phoneme*

Show the children several mounted pictures with the names clearly printed below the picture, such as *car, scarf, park, farm, barn, cart, garden, market, farmer.* Four or five of these pictures placed where the children can see them are sufficient.
Note: This is the first combination of a vowel with **r.** The sound of **a** is slightly altered. The same **a** sound appears in **father.** The slightly altered **a** is not what is commonly known as a "modified vowel." This term properly applies to the vowels in **her, word, bird, fur,** and **cedar.**

Procedure

*recognizing the grapheme for the **ar** phoneme*

Help the children identify the pictures, having them say the words after you. Ask, "What sound did you hear in every word?" After the correct response has been given, have the children look at each word. "What do you see that is the same in each word?" (*ar*) Explain that the letters **ar** say the **ar** sound that the children hear. Have several children frame the sound with their hands. List on the board the words from the book, and have the children read the words and draw a line around the **ar** sounds. Put **are** in sentences:

Tag and Rags *are* pets.
Ned and Tom *are* fat.

introducing the word are

Discuss **are,** explaining that the **e** is silent. This is a slightly irregular spelling because the silent **e** does not change the vowel sound. The children will read the word **are** in context.

Use of Text

reviewing the care of books

1. Direct the children to look at their new books; discuss the cover, the title, and the table of contents. Give the children several

minutes to look through the book, glancing at the pictures, etc., before having them turn to page 1.

2. Have the children look at the illustration, having them recall the **ar** sound. Use **cart** as a reference if they have difficulty. Ask what other objects they see in the picture that have this sound. (*star, arms, scarf*)

3. Give the children several seconds to look over the **words** under the picture. Call on individuals to read each word.

checking vocabulary comprehension

4. Review the words by having the children find as fast as possible: (1) a place where animals live (*farm*); (2) something to wear (*scarf*); (3) something you send on someone's birthday (*card*); (4) a part of your body (*arm*), etc.

5. Dictate the word **part.** Have one child write this on the board; a second, change it to **smart;** a third, change **smart** to **dart;** next, change **dart** to **mart,** and so on, using **mar, car, card, cart,** and **art.**

Suggestions for Further Activities

reinforcing the **ar** phoneme through vocabulary development

1. Have the children build a list of words using the **ar** sound, such as:

part
dart
mart
smart

If you have letter boxes, they can be used here to build words; otherwise the children can print them. If this exercise is used, be sure the board is erased after the class lesson.

providing exercises for independent work

2. Have the children illustrate eight words out of a list of twelve, choosing the ones they wish to use and writing the word beneath each picture.

3. Give the children a duplicated sheet of sentences where **are** appears many times. Have the children underline or draw a line around the word. Put **are** on the board or expose the flash card for those who need to refer to it.

Duplicating Master No. 1 gives practice in recognition of **are.**

Workbook page 1 may also follow this lesson.

Page 2 — The Cats and the Cart

Introduction

presenting a story using the **ar** phoneme

Have the children look at the picture and help them to identify Tom as a worker of some sort. Have them observe that Tom is loadings eggs on a cart. Give the children an opportunity to read the sign silently, and then call on a child to read the sign attached to the cart.

Guiding Reading for Comprehension

Discuss the title of the story with the children. Have the children read the first line to themselves to answer the questions, "What kind of worker is Tom? What does he do?" (*farm hand*) After a child has answered the questions (do not have the child read the entire line, but encourage him to answer only the questions asked), have another child read the line smoothly. Tell the children to look at the second line and then have them read to find out what kind of cart the farm hand has. (*farm cart*) Follow the same procedure as before, getting an answer to the direct question first and then having the sentence read. Continue to the third sentence and ask, "What is on the cart? Put your finger under the word that tells what is on the cart." (*card*) Check the responses and have the sentence read orally. In the last sentence, direct the children to put their fingers under the word that tells what Tom is putting into his cart. (*eggs*) (If questions were asked for these last two sentences, the children could answer by looking at the pictures. Having them locate the answer and point to it avoids this.) After all four lines have been studied, have a child read the entire page for continuity before going on to page 3.

checking comprehension

Page 3 — The Cats and the Cart (*continued*)

Guiding Reading for Comprehension

The procedure for page 3 is similar to page 2. A brief discussion of the picture should bring out the suspense of what might be going to happen. Give the children an opportunity to tell what they think might be the end of the story.

building motivation through suspense

Look at the text, and ask, "Where is Tom going? (*off*) What will he get? (*a tart*) Read the second sentence and tell why Tom doesn't hear the cats. (*Tom is far*) Read the third sentence and frame *at the cart*. Look at the whole page and frame *from the cart, to get a tart, Tom runs, Tom is far.*"

After this opportunity for the children to become familiar with the words, call on a child to read the entire page. Work for fluency and continuity.

Page 4 — The Cats and the Cart (*conclusion*)

Guiding Reading for Comprehension

enjoying the humor of the story

On page 4, let the children enjoy the humor of the story as shown by the picture. Call attention to the question in the story. Let the children read silently before calling on a child to read the question. Direct them to the answer in the second sentence and the climax in the final sentence. After having each sentence read aloud, have the entire page read for continuity.

It is suggested that the entire story be read aloud for enjoyment.

Suggestions for Further Activities

using nonsense jingles for vocabulary development

Put nonsense jingles on the board to be illustrated. The children may do all, or may choose one and do a larger illustration. Either the teacher or a child may print the jingles for a display.

A cat in a cart
Is not smart.

A part of a tart
Is in the cart.

The fast red car
Runs far to a star.

Pat hit his arm.
It did not harm.

Duplicating Master No. 2 can be used here.
Workbook pages 2 and 3 follow this lesson.

Enrichment

providing enrichment activities

Aesop, "Belling the Cat," in *Arbuthnot Anthology of Children's Literature,* Scott, Foresman.
Flack, Marjorie, *Angus and the Cat,* Doubleday.
Gag, Wanda, *Millions of Cats,* Coward-McCann.
Jackson, Kathryn and Byron, *Big Farmer Big and Little Farmer Little,* Simon.

Pages 5, 6, 7, and 8 — Two-syllable words

her

Introduction

introducing two-syllable words

Play a listening game, having the children clap once as you say, **fast;** then clap twice as you say, **fast er;** continue with **farm, farmer,**

start, started, and **dent, dented.** Pronounce these words carefully so that the children will hear both syllables, but pronounce them without distorting the words.

Procedure—Auditory Exercises

As the children clap, explain that each syllable has a sound by itself, almost like a word, as it sometimes is. Continue having the children clap, but have them determine whether they hear a one-syllable or two-syllable word as you read the list:

performing auditory discrimination

damper	hunter	pepper	truck
dump	hunted	into	handed
mend	dart	hand	camper

Visual Exercises

Direct the children to open their books to page 5 and notice the illustration of the farmer. Put the word **farmer** on the board. Have the children pronounce it and discover whether the word has one or two syllables. Put a *2* after the word. Return to the picture and ask what the farmer will do. (*farm*) Put this word on the board after the children have clapped their hands to determine the number of syllables. Place a *1* after the word. Ask the children to underline the vowels in **farmer.** (*They find 2.*) Then ask them to underline the vowels in **farm.** (*They find 1.*) Explain that every syllable must have a vowel. It can have more than one, but it must have at least one. When the vowels that we hear are separated by consonants, we have a two-syllable word.

visual discrimination of two syllables

Return to the text and have the children read the words with the **er** ending. After you have presented **hunter,** the children should not have much difficulty with the **er** sound. If they do, put several of the words on the board and move your hand across under the words as you pronounce **faster, farmer, starter, tender.** Put some of these words in simple sentences on the board so that the phoneme-grapheme pattern taught is applied immediately to oral reading. For example:

Tom ran faster and faster.
The farmer fed the pigs.

Have the children find the two-syllable words and underline them. Also have them draw a line around the two vowels in each.

Procedure for Special Word

After reading the **er** two-syllable words, call attention to the word **her.** Try to get a child's response. It may be necessary to have him cover **h,** discover **er,** and add **h.** Before leaving this word, ask how

presenting the special word *her*

many syllables there are in it. The word **her** is special because it has only one syllable in a group of two-syllable words. It is not an irregular word.
Note: It may be desirable to end the lesson here and spend time in reviewing the words presented.

Page 4 of the accompanying workbook may be used following this lesson.

Procedure for Page 6

introducing the suffix *ed* pronounced as a syllable

Follow the same procedure with the **ed** words on page 6. Before reading the two-syllable words which are not formed by a suffix, explain that all two-syllable words are not formed by adding an ending to a whole word. Some words start as two syllables. Progress slowly, helping the children to see two syllables before reading a word aloud. Avoid having the children pronounce one syllable before they are ready to read the entire word.

Use these two-syllable words in simple sentences on the board so that the phoneme-grapheme patterns taught are applied immediately to oral reading. For example:

Ted started the car.
Ann mended her rug.
Ted has a garden.
The camper put up his tent.
The hunter is in the forest.

Have the children find the two-syllable words and underline them. Also, have them draw a line around the two vowels.
Note: The word *into* does not contain two short vowels but **to** was introduced as a special word in *Book A* so the introduction of the word here should present no special difficulty.

Procedure for Pages 7 and 8

introducing the alternate pronunciation of the *ed* syllable

In introducing the words on pages 7 and 8, tell the children that some words that end in **ed** do not have two syllables. The ending of these words sounds like **d** or **t** instead of **ed.** Do not dwell on these pronunciations as they are quite natural to the child and will not present a problem in context. These endings will be discussed in more depth in *Book C,* pages 44 through 47.

Suggestions for Further Activities

reinforcing syllabic discrimination

1. Put two-syllable words on a mimeographed sheet; have the children find the vowels.

2. On a mimeographed sheet, list one-syllable and two-syllable words at random. Have the children put a *1* or *2* in front of each word, depending on the number of syllables they see in it.

Example: 2 tender
1 mark
2 harder

Duplicating Master No. 3 is similar to the above.
Workbook page 5 may follow this lesson.

Enrichment

providing enrichment activities

Some simple nursery rhymes, like "Little Miss Muffet," "Little Jack Horner," "Lucy Locket," and "Little Tommy Tucker," may be said in unison, with the children clapping rhythmically. The titles may be repeated slowly so that the children recognize two-syllable words.

Page 9 — The sound of w

Building Linguistic Skills

phoneme-grapheme relationship

The recognition of **w** as an initial sound.

Introduction

introduction of the initial **w** phoneme

Say, "See the inch worm wiggle,
Wiggle, wiggle, wind.
Such a humpy, bumpy traveler
We will never find."

Repeat the jingle and have the children say it after you.

Procedure

providing auditory discrimination activities

1. Repeat **wiggle, wiggle, wind,** exaggerating the **w** sound. Point out **w** in the alphabet and ask a child to name the letter.

2. Have the children turn to page 9. Say, "Wagon—Notice that **wagon** and **wiggle** start with the same sound. The initial letter is **w.**"

3. Say the following words, having the children repeat them after you:

want	won't	wake	wet
will	water	wear	wait
weather	way	wind	witch

4. Do any discriminatory exercises, having the children hear like sounds or unlike sounds. Here are some suggested groups of words:

wag	west	we	wear	wig
will	sun	weak	gown	pig
yell	wind	bend	warm	went

building vocabulary through riddles

5. Here are some simple riddles to use, if desired:

I help to fly kites.
I make sailboats go.
Mothers like me to help
dry clothes.
I am the (*wind*).

I am a toy.
Boys ride in me.
I can be used to
help mother.
I am a (*wagon*).

I tell what the flag does
when the wind blows.
I also tell what children jump
in at the beach.
Children make me with their hands
when they say goodbye.
I am the word (*wave*).

I am something wet.
Children like to play in me.
I help things to float.
I make people healthy, too.
I am (*water*).

---

reviewing two-syllable words

6. Have the children read the words in the list on page 9. It may be necessary to review one of the two-syllable words, like **faster,** to recall **er** if the children have any difficulty. In this case, put **faster** on the board and review the **er** sound. Then put **winter** on the board and develop it as another word. After this, **western** can be developed from **west.** Say, "Find the **er** sound in this word," so that the children are prepared for this element and can study and pronounce the word as a whole, rather than sounding it out painfully in parts. After **winter** and **western** are taught, **were** should present no problem if the teacher explains that the last **e** is silent. She either covers it with her hand, or draws a line through it on the board so that the children see only **wer.**

7. Put words in sentences either on the board or the card holder:

The farmer has a red wagon.
Tom has mittens for winter.

presenting the word *mittens*

Note: The word **mittens** has no new sound or spelling; therefore, although the children may need guidance, they should have no real difficulty. Be sure to give ample time for silent study.

The west wind is soft.
Ned's arms are wet.

Nan went to a western farm.
Did Ann win a wig?

Call on individual children to read the sentences. Call on the children to underline and read the words beginning with **w.** (In meeting individual differences, it is important to call on children who are progressing slowly to read the less difficult sentences. There will be ample opportunity for them to do increasingly difficult work as the year goes on.)

Suggestions for Further Activities

independent exercises for visual and auditory discrimination

1. Some of these words have a variety of meanings; this is, therefore, an excellent time to have children illustrate words beginning with **w.** These do not have to be words the children can read, as long as they can tell you what the words represent, such as: **wave, wind** (long or short **i**), **wet, water, west, wig, wag, win.** There are many possibilities for vocabulary enrichment here, and this should never be overlooked. Assign four pictures of anything they can think of that begins with **w.**
2. Have the children find four magazine pictures of objects whose names begin with **w.**
3. Put the following sentences on the board to be illustrated:

   1. Ted's arms are wet.
   2. Ed has a red wagon.
   3. The pig is in a wig.
   4. The car went fast.

Workbook page 6 follows this lesson.

Enrichment

providing enrichment activities

Read any stories or poems about the wind—for example:
"Who Has Seen the Wind," by Christina Rossetti, in *Time for Poetry*, Scott, Foresman.
"Wind on the Hill," by A. A. Milne, in *Now We Are Six*, Dutton.
"The Wind and the Sun," *Aesop's Fables*, Lippincott.

Page 10 — Pat and the Wagon

Introduction

motivating through a picture

Begin the story by discussing the picture. Ask what season it is. (*winter*) Have the children describe the picture. Ask why they think the boys and the dog are running. Encourage them to use their imaginations. Then tell them we must read to find out.

Guiding Reading for Comprehension

checking comprehension

Tell the children to read the first sentence silently. Then have them frame the word that tells the season. (*winter*) Ask them what the grass was like. (*wet*) Make sure that they understand why the grass was wet. (*winter snow*) Ask them to read the second sentence to find the name of the first boy. (*Sam*) Then ask where Sam went. (*into the garden*) Ask them what word tells how Sam went into the garden. (*darted*) Have these two sentences read aloud by several children.

developing smooth oral reading

Have the children read the third sentence to find the name of the second boy. (*Win*) What did Win do? (*started to run*) Then proceed to read the final sentence to find the name of the dog. (*Wag*) Where did Wag go? (*to Win*) How did he go? (*fast*) Before going on to the next page, have the entire page read aloud. Several children should have the opportunity to read aloud.

Page 11 — Pat and the Wagon (*continued*)

Guiding Reading for Comprehension

recognizing reasons for actions

Another character is introduced here. Have the children read the first sentence to find who the new character is. (*Pat, the cat*) Where is Pat? (*in the wagon*) Look at the picture now and ask if Pat looks happy? (*no*) Why do they think Pat looks unhappy? Discuss how cats react to water.

reading to answer questions

developing two meanings of *fast*

Continue developing comprehension with questions for the rest of the page. Ask, "What happened to the wagon?" (*ran into wet sand*) Discuss the children's personal experiences with trying to pull something through wet sand. Bring out the difficulty of moving something stuck in wet sand. For the third sentence, ask what the wet sand is like. (*not hard*) Finally, ask what the wagon did in the wet sand. (*dug in fast*) You may need to bring out the meaning of *fast* used in this way.

Page 12 — Pat and the Wagon (*continued*)

Introduction

Have the children look at the picture and discuss the emotions of the boys, and the reactions of the dog and the cat. Build interest in the situation.

recognizing emotions

Guiding Reading for Comprehension

Read the first sentence to see where Sam was. (*at the wagon*) Who was there with him? (*Win and Wag*) Have these two sentences read aloud. In the third sentence ask the class to find the word that describes Pat. (*sad*) "How sad was Pat?" (*sad as a winter sun*) You may need to develop this comparison with the children. Why do they think a winter sun is sad? Ask what happens in the last sentence to the wagon. (*crept in faster*)

developing abstract comparisons

Page 13 — Pat and the Wagon (*conclusion*)

Guiding Reading for Comprehension

Go right on with the story. Ask what the boys and dog did. (*dug in*) You may need to explain this expression. Ask, "What happened to the wagon?" (*started up*) "Where was Pat?" (*on the wagon*) "Did Pat get to the garden?" (*yes*)

Now go back and enjoy with the pupils the picture at the top of this page. Bring out the humor of the picture—the boys tugging, the dog pulling, and the cat urging them on.

recognizing humor in the story

Have the children read this last page aloud. Then, if it seems desirable, go back and have the entire story read aloud. You may conclude with a discussion of any particular phase of the story that seems to fascinate your group: the wagon getting stuck in the mud, the cat not getting out into the water and swimming, the help of a pet. Have the children relate their own experiences.

relating personal experiences to the story

Suggestions for Further Activities

1. Put the following sentences on the board, having the children fill in each blank with a word from the word list. This is an oral group activity.

providing an exercise for independent study

1. Sam darted into the __________.
2. __________ sat on the wagon.
3. Wet sand is not __________.
4. Pat got as sad as a __________ sun.
5. Sam and Win and Wag __________ in.
6. The __________ started up.

wagon
Sam
winter
hard
garden
sand
Pat
dug
got

2. A similar exercise can be duplicated for independent work, with children writing the correct word.

Enrichment

providing enrichment activities

Use any stories you like about wagons. For example:

Allen, Marie Louise, "Jim and Scotch and the Little Red Wagon," in *Tales Told Under the Blue Umbrella,* The Macmillan Company.

Baruch, Dorothy, "The Express Wagon," in *Tales Told Under the Blue Umbrella,* The Macmillan Company.

Cording, Ruth, "Luke and His Little Red Wagon," in *Read Me More Stories,* Thomas Y. Crowell Company.

Page 14 — Sound of wa

phoneme-grapheme relationships

Building Linguistic Skills

Recognition of the sound of **a** when preceded by **w.**

Introduction

Use a picture of water; i.e., a beach, ocean, pool, etc.

Procedure

introducing the **wa** pattern

Print the word **water,** or even the entire sentence, *"It is fun to swim in the water,"* under the picture. Call on the children to read the sentence, and then to find the word **water.** After several have framed **water** (also *swim*), print it on the board or show the flash card and call the children's attention to the spelling. The children will hear the new sound of **a.** Explain that many times, with **w,** the **a** sounds almost like **o.** Put some of the words on the board from page 14, having the children read each one as you put it on. Develop **wart, warm,** and **swarm** from **war.** Do not neglect the meanings of these words. Point out that the **w** may come before or after the **a** to change the sound, but also bring out that it does not always change it, as in **wagon** and **wag.** Continue developing all the words; then, in addition, use them with short vowel words in simple phrases or sentences:

using the **wa** pattern in phrases

I want a wagon.	Pat wants a pet.
war in the west	A swarm of wasps
a warm wind	Water is warm.
Warren is wet.	Was the water warm?
Ned was warm.	Was the wagon red?
The car was red.	Was it a west wind?
It went fast.	

Have the children take turns reading the phrases and sentences; then pronounce a single word and have a child frame it and pronounce it. If you think it is needed for fluency, have the child, or another child, read the entire phrase containing the word.

Incidentally, in oral reading, bring out the common pronunciation of **was.** Run your hand across from left to right to prevent confusion of **was** and **saw.**

preventing confusion of *was* and *saw*

Suggestions for Further Activities

providing independent exercises

1. If some of the suggestions on page 9 were not done at this time, they could be used here.
2. Simple phrases or sentences can be copied and illustrated:

a red wagon	a warm hat
in the water	Wag is a dog.

Page 15 — Ted and Rags

Introduction

Discuss the picture, having the children see the happy expression on Rags' face and the mixed emotions which Ted is experiencing. Discuss why Ted feels as he does, etc.

interpreting emotions of story characters

Guiding Reading for Comprehension

Have the children read silently to find out whom the story is about. (*Ted and Rags*) Ask, "What is the title?" (*Ted and Rags*) "Who can find a word beginning with *w*?" (*water*) Have the children

finding the title

oral reading for continuity

locate and read these words. Ask, "How does the water feel?" (*warm*) "What did Ted want to do?" (*run in the water*) "What did he *not* want to do?" (*get wet*) "What happened to Rags?" (*got wetter and wetter*) After these questions for silent reading have been asked, have several children read the page aloud. Divide the text into three parts and have individual children read each part; then have one child read the entire page for continuity.

Page 16 — Ted and Rags (*continued*)

said

Introduction

relating personal experiences

In the discussion of the picture, give one or two children an opportunity to relate similar personal experiences.

Guiding Reading for Comprehension

developing punctuation skills: quotation marks

Explain that quotation marks show the exact words someone has said. Ask, "What did Ted say to Rags?" (*Get it, Rags, get it*) Have the children read the words between the quotation marks, first silently, then orally, emphasizing expression. Say, "Read the way you would say it if Rags were your dog." Ask the children who they think said these words. As they respond (*Ted*), explain that this is just what the story says. Read the first sentence for them.

oral reading with expression

Continue to develop expressive reading by asking the children to study the second sentence and read it the way they think Ted said it. Let several children read it the way they would say it.

Finish the page by having the children read silently to find out what happened to Rags. (*got wetter and wetter*) Call on individuals to read each sentence. One of the better readers can probably be allowed to read the entire page.

Before going on, ask the children what the special word is at the bottom of the page. (*said*)

Pages 17 and 18 — Ted and Rags (*continued*)

Introduction

seeing humor in the picture

Discuss whether Rags got the gun. Recall that Ted did not want to get wet, and call attention to the humor from this present situation in the picture.

Guiding Reading for Comprehension

Have the children read the first two sentences. Ask who got the gun (*Rags*) and where Ted went. (*to Rags*) In presenting the next sentences, ask what Rags did. (*got the water off*)

reviewing quotation marks

On page 18 ask where the water went. (*from Rags to Ted*) Have the children look for quotation marks. Ask who said the words. (*Ted*) Review the special word *said*. In the last sentences, ask what Ted said about the water and how it felt. (*wet and warm*)

developing good oral expression

Follow the same plan for oral reading. These two pages may be too long for some children to read. The story is a good one to re-read to develop good oral expression.

Discuss the humor of the story and the children's personal experiences. It is better to allow free discussion before or after the story rather than risk breaking up the continuity in the middle of the story.

developing creative writing

Other activities may include illustrations of the children's own stories. They may dictate short experiences with their pets, funny things that have happened, or any similar stories, which the teacher prints under each child's picture.

Procedure for Special Word

reinforcing the special word *said*

This exercise to reinforce the word **said** may be introduced following the oral reading, or it may be a separate lesson.

Put **said Ted** on the board. Under it, put **Ted said,** and have a child read each one. Add **Pam said,** or use names of the children in the group, writing the word **said** several times. Have the group read these phrases before returning to the book, page 16.

Have a child read the entire first sentence. Have the children study the second sentence and then read it with much expression.

Suggestions for Further Activities

exercises for independent work

1. Have the children write the word **said** in the blanks. This work may be copied from the board for a writing lesson, or duplicated.

said

Tom _____, "Run, Nan, run fast."
"Nan can run fast," _____ Ned.
"Run, Ann," _____ Ed. "Run faster."
"Ann did win," Tom _____.

Be sure to have the children read the sentences orally, either before or after they have written **said.**

Note: At this time, it is not necessary to emphasize the placement of a comma or a period before the quotation marks in a sentence.

2. Give the children opportunities to practice writing letters, and, in some cases, to illustrate them. Regular lined writing paper

developing kinesthetic skills

should be given them if they are to copy from the board, or duplicated material should provide lines with proper spacing. Example:

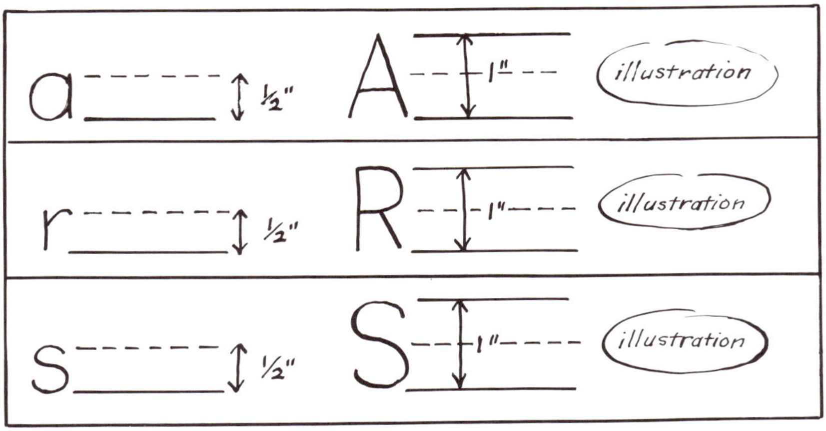

Workbook page 7 follows this lesson.
Duplicating Master No. 4 may be used here.

Enrichment

providing enrichment activities

Here is another opportunity for any of the fine dog stories or poems which the children have, or which are suggested in the bibliography.

Teach the children to play the game "Little Sally Waters."

Page 19 — Sound of aw

phoneme-grapheme relationships

Building Linguistic Skills

The sound of **a** when followed by **w**.

Introduction

introducing the word *saw* and the **aw** pattern

A picture can be used here to illustrate a dog's paw, a fawn, or any of the words listed. If these pictures are difficult to find, use three or four mounted pictures of objects. Flash very quickly; then say, "What did you see?" The child will answer, "I saw a cat," or "I saw a _____" (whatever he could see in the rapid exposure). Print his response on the board: "Ned saw a cat." Expose another picture and repeat the question, and again have the child respond,

"I saw _____." Again put it on the board: "Jack saw a _____." After several sentences have been put on the board, have the children find and frame **saw**.

If the pictures are used, print under the picture (or over, if picture is on chalkboard) simple sentences, such as: *The dog's paw is tan. A fawn is in the forest.* Give the children time to study the picture and sentence before reading it. Have a child find **fawn** (or **paw**).

practicing auditory discrimination of the **aw** pattern

Recall with the children that **a** preceded by **w** sounds almost like (short) **o.** It does also when followed by **w.** Dictate a few simple words to be written on the board, such as *saw, dawn, draw.* Then have the children turn to the texts and read the words.

Use **saw** and **was** in sentences on the board. Run your hand from left to right under the words to help avoid confusions.

reinforcing *saw* and *was*

Ted saw a cat.
The cat was tan.
Pam saw a car.
The car was red.
The hunter saw a fawn.
The fawn was in the forest.
The fawn saw the hunter.
The fawn was fast.

Suggestions for Further Activities

Put the following sentences on the board for a written exercise, or duplicate them. Read and fill in the blank in the first sentence with the children.

exercises for independent work

saw **was**

1. Nan _____ a cat.
2. It _____ a pet cat.
3. It _____ in a hat.
4. The cat _____ Nan.
5. Nan _____ it run fast.

Workbook page 8 follows this lesson.
Duplicating Master No. 5 can be used here.

Page 20 — A Fawn at Dawn

Introduction

Have the children look at the picture on page 20. Ask what animal they see. (*a fawn*) If no one knows, you may tell them. Tell developing animal vocabulary

them that a fawn is a baby animal. Ask what animal it will be when it grows up. *(deer)* If time permits, you may discuss names for other baby animals that are different from their adult names. Some examples might be: **lamb—sheep; calf—cow; kitten—cat; puppy—dog; colt—horse.**

Guiding Reading for Comprehension

reading to answer questions

Have a child read the title. Ask what time of the day it is. (*dawn*) Have the pupils read the first sentence silently. Then ask what the boys' names are. (*Sam, Win*) Ask what Sam handed Win. (*a gun*) Have them read the second sentence to find what Win handed Sam. (*a dart*) Have a child read these two sentences. Ask the children why they think Sam and Win have a gun and a dart. Build suspense.

Have the children read the next two sentences. Ask, "Where did Sam and Win go?" (*into the forest*) "What was in the forest?" (*fawns*) Have these sentences read orally. Someone may read the whole page, if you wish.

Page 21 — A Fawn at Dawn (*continued*)

Guiding Reading for Comprehension

checking comprehension

Continue with questions to develop page 21 with a procedure similar to the one used for page 20. Ask questions such as, "What did Win see?" (*a fawn*) "What word describes the fawn?" (*fat*) "When did he see it?" (*at dawn*) You may wish to have the children frame the words *fawn* and *dawn* when they answer the questions. "Did the fawn see Sam and Win?" (*yes*) Have the sentences read orally. "What did the fawn do?" (*run*) Have them frame the word that tells how the fawn ran. (*fast*) "Where did it run?" (*under the winter camp tent*)

Page22 — A Fawn at Dawn (*continued*)

Introduction

using the picture to motivate reading

Discuss the picture. Ask the children where they think the fawn is. Ask them if they think Sam and Win will find it. Read the page to find out.

Guiding Reading for Comprehension

Have the children read the first sentence silently to find out what Sam and Win did. (*hunted the fawn*) Ask the children to read the next sentence and tell where the fawn was. (*in the tent*) In the third sentence, ask "What did Sam do then?" (*started to the farm*) Ask the children why he is going to the farm. (*couldn't find the fawn*) Have them read the last sentence aloud.

reading for comprehension

Page 23 — A Fawn at Dawn (*conclusion*)

Guiding Reading for Comprehension

Continue right on to the end of the story by asking questions. Ask, "Where did Win and Sam go?" (*to the farm*) "Why did Win want to go?" (*to get warm*) "What season was it?" (*winter*) Have someone read the third sentence that tells what the winter did to Win. Finally, ask, "Did Win and Sam hurt the fawn?" (*no*) Review the entire story by having it read aloud. Call on several students so that all may participate as often as possible.

Now you may want to bring out the moral in the story. Have the pupils go back to page 22 and read the last sentence. (*Sam must not harm the fawn.*) Then have them read the last sentence on page 23. (*Win and Sam did not harm the fawn.*) Have the children discuss why the boys did not harm the fawn. Was it because they did not want to be cruel? Or did they really love animals? Or was it because they could not catch the fawn and they were getting very cold? Try to have the children bring out these alternatives instead of suggesting them yourself.

drawing a conclusion by inference

recognizing reasons for actions

A natural conclusion to this story would be a discussion of taking care of animals. The children will be familiar with taking care of pets, but here you may bring out how we take care of animals in the forest. Also discuss how these animals find ways to protect themselves. Bring out the fact that the fawn hid because it was afraid. Animals are often afraid of people; that is why they run from us. Have the children share their personal experiences with animals in the park, camping, etc.

creative expression: discussing personal experiences

Suggestions for Further Activities

1. Make a duplicated sheet like the one that follows. Have the children underline those sentences that are true. If you prefer, these sentences could be put on the board and the comprehension exercise could be combined with a writing lesson.

providing an exercise for independent study

1. Win handed Sam a gun.
2. Win handed Sam a dart.
3. Sam and Win went into the forest.
4. Cats were in the forest.
5. The fawn ran to the farm.
6. Sam and Win went into the tent.
7. Sam harmed the fawn.
8. It was winter.

using pictures for a bulletin board display

2. Have the children draw or look for pictures of animals in magazines. Classify these animals as wild animals or pets. This project could make an attractive bulletin board display.

Enrichment

providing enrichment

Salton, Felix, *Bambi*.

Page 24 — Special sound of ow as in cow

Building Linguistic Skills

phoneme-grapheme relationships

One sound of **o** when followed by **w.** Phoneme-grapheme pattern as heard in **cow.**

Introduction

introducing the **ow** pattern

Allow the children to enjoy the humor in the picture and ask what they think this little "engine" is saying. What do they say when they pinch their fingers or stub their toes? (*ow*)

Procedure

practicing auditory recognition of the **ow** pattern

Put **ow** on the board and call on a child to "make it say **how.**" Call on another child to change it (or rewrite it) to **now.** Continue through the five words **how, now, cow, down,** and **town.**

Put on the board for practice in reading aloud fluently:

a tan cow
down town
how fast
down to the farm
starts now
saw a cow

Use flashcards for rapid drill.

Workbook page 9 may be used here.

Pages 24 and 25 — The Cow and the Frog

Introduction

The illustration for this story is humorous enough to serve as motivation. Discuss the comical situation and ask what the children think will happen next, and why. Ask, "Can the cow swim? Can the frog swim?"

using humor as motivation for reading

Guiding Reading for Comprehension

Have the children read the title silently, and then aloud. This will reinforce the **ow** sound previously learned.

reinforcing the **ow** pattern

Questions for guided reading: "Where was the frog sitting?" (*on a raft*) (This cannot be guessed from the picture.) "Who saw the frog? (*a tan cow*) What did the cow do?" (*sat down*) (These three sentences may be read aloud as a thought unit at this point if the teacher so desires.) "What happened to the raft? Find the word that tells in which direction it went." (*down*) "Now find the word that tells where the cow is sitting." (*water*)

checking comprehension

Direct the children to read the last sentence so that they can read the entire story smoothly.

Have several children read the story aloud for pleasure as well as for fluency and expression.

Workbook page 10 follows this lesson.

Here is an opportunity to encourage original, imaginative stories. Nonsense stories, rhymes, and jingles can provoke creativity as well as appreciation for this type of literature.

encouraging creativity

Page 26 — Words with the l sound

Building Linguistic Skills

The sound of **l** as an initial consonant, and as part of an initial blend. The sound of **l** in medial and terminal positions.

phoneme-grapheme relationships

Introduction

In learning the nursery rhymes, the children may have recited or sung, "Mary Had a Little Lamb." If so, have them recite it again, showing them a picture of a little lamb from a farm storybook or from your own collection. If they are not familiar with the rhyme, teach or read it now.

Procedure

introducing the initial **l** phoneme

1. Repeat **little lamb,** having the children repeat after you several times.

2. Instead of reading the list of words on page 26 and having the children repeat them, for variety have them rhyme with the words in the list. Say, "bag," and have the child respond, "lag." Explain that all the words must begin like **lamb.** Other words to use:

practice in rhyming words

bad	beg	tint
hog	rip	fist
cap	fast	frost
wet	mess	pain

3. Have a child point to **l** in the alphabet. Then dictate some of the three-letter words that begin with **l** for board work or for written exercises.

recognizing the **l** phoneme in a medial position

4. Call one child to the board, explain that this is going to be more difficult, and have the entire class watch as you dictate **clap.** (The meaning of **clap** is easier for all children, probably, than **clam** or **clan.**) After all the children have seen the initial blend, continue dictating, using the words from the book. These words should be developed while all the children watch the child at the board so that all of the blends will be seen and heard by everyone.

developing writing skills

5. As these words are spelled, make a duplicate list higher on the board or arrange a duplicate list of flash cards in the card holder. Use this as a review, having the children find dictated words after the writing part of the lesson has been completed. (This writing can slow the lesson down and cause it to lag. If this is the case, dictate some words from each blend group, and then develop the remainder of the list without the writing experiences.) Use the words in sentences frequently; for instance—"Find **clam. Clams** live in the sand under the water and they are good to eat. Find **clam.**" "Find **plug.** I will put a **plug** in the sink so the water won't go away. Find **plug.**"

Note: In developing the lesson, the teacher should include as many, or as few, of the words from the book as necessary for the particular group.

recognizing initial, medial, and terminal sounds

6. After the words have been reviewed several times visually, remove the list and have the children listen and locate the initial, medial, and terminal sounds. There are a variety of ways that this may be done:

a) Say, "log"; ask, "What is the first sound? What is the name of the first letter?"
b) Say, "class"; ask, "What is the last sound?"
c) Say, "glad"; ask, "What is the last letter?"
d) Say, "flat"; ask, "What is the vowel sound in the middle?"
e) Say, "slip"; ask, "What is the name of the vowel in the middle?"

Use the terms *sound* and *name of the letter,* as well as *first, last, middle,* and *vowel.*

Suggestions for Further Activities

exercises for independent work

1. Have the children:
   a) find four things that begin with **l** in magazines.
   b) draw four things that begin with **l**.

2. Write the following list on the board and have the children complete the words. Be sure that the children understand that these must be real words that they can read. If the children make words which have not been listed, this should, of course, be praised.

gla__	l__st	cl__p	lo__
fl__p	__ap	pl__g	sla__

Duplicating Master No. 6 can be used here.
Workbook pages 11 and 12 can also follow this lesson.

Enrichment

providing enrichment activities

Poem: de la Mare, Walter, "The Cupboard," in Arbuthnot, *Time for Poetry,* Scott, Foresman.

Nursery Rhyme: "Lucy Locket," in *Anthology of Children's Literature,* Houghton Mifflin.

Story: "The Lion and the Mouse," in *Aesop's Fables,* Lippincott.

Page 27 — Words having double l

Building Linguistic Skills

phoneme-grapheme relationships

The double **ll** at the end of the word and the exceptional phoneme resulting from **ull.**

Introduction

teaching a nursery rhyme

Have the nursery rhyme "Jack and Jill" printed on a chart so that the children can see it, or have them recite it. If they can see it, have them read it in unison. Have them find, or recall, all the words that end in an **l** sound. List these words on the board.

Procedure

introducing the **ll** pattern for the **l** phoneme

1. After you have listed *Jill, hill,* and *fell,* ask if someone notices anything unusual. Call attention, if necessary, to the double **l**.

2. Have the children open their books to page 27. Explain that just as the sound of **a** is changed or modified by a **w**, it is also changed when followed by an **l**. Put the word **saw** on the board and have it read. Ask for the sound of **a** in **saw**.

3. Direct the children's attention to the first word on the page. Call on various children to read the first three lines of words. They should present no difficulty.

teaching the irregular **ull** pattern

4. Treat the irregular words—*pull, full,* and *pullet,* as follows: Put the following sentence on the board:

Put the log down.

Have a child read it aloud for the class. Explain that there is something else you could do to the log. Change **put** to **pull**. Have this read. Erase the remainder of the sentence. Have a child recall **pull**; then change it to **full**. Put **full** in a sentence, *The pan is full,* and have it read aloud. Put **pull** on the board again, recall it, and change it to **pullet**. Explain that a "pullet is a small hen." Put the sentence on the board. Explain that there are a few words that have a different sound for **u** and review **put**, **pull**, **full**, and **pullet** with flash cards for two or three minutes.

Modifications of *a* with *l* and *ll*

introducing the modified **a** with **l** and **ll**

Reread to the children, *A pullet is a small hen.* Have the children find words with **l's** and underline them. When someone has underlined **small**, reread it, or have a child read it as you move your hand under the sentence so that everyone will recognize **small**. Ask what the name of the vowel is. It is enough now to recall that other letters (**r** and **w**) changed the sound of **a**, and **l** can change it too. Discuss with the children, the sentences with the modified words on page 27, using the board, and having them find and frame the words as you say them.

Suggestions for Further Activities

providing exercises for independent work

1. Have the children illustrate phrases or sentences using words beginning or ending with **l**, such as:

a lad at the mill
The flag has a slit.
a plant on the wall
Pull the log up the hill.

2. Use Duplicating Master No. 7 or put simple sketches on a duplicated sheet and supply part of the word. Have the children complete the word. Here is an example:

ditto

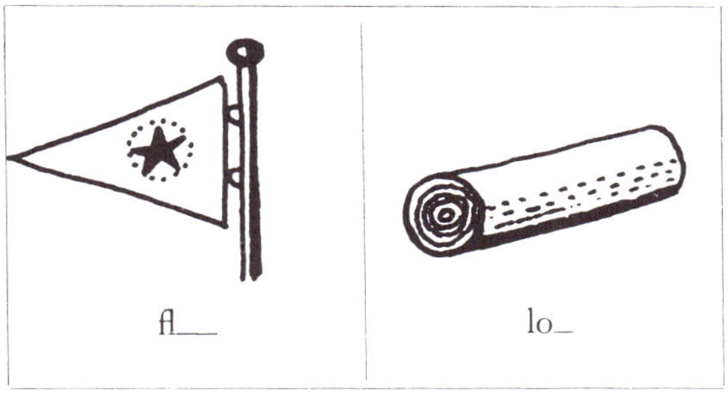

Enrichment

providing enrichment

Use the poem on page 28 for enrichment.

Page 28 — A poem: Ellen on a hill-top

Introduction

enjoying a poem

This simple lyrical poem creates a picture, not a story.

Procedure

locating the ll pattern

1. Allow the children an opportunity to read the poem silently. Have them locate all the words having double l's. List these words

checking comprehension

developing a sense of rhythm for poetry

on the board and review them so that the poem will present no difficulty when read.

2. Ask what the little girl's name is. Ask where she is. (*Ellen, on a hill-top*)
3. Have the group read the poem in unison.
4. Have several children read it aloud alone.
5. Ask why the word **still** is repeated. If no one can answer, reread it to the group, and as you reread it, have the children clap their hands lightly, feeling the rhythm. They will feel the need for three syllables at the end.
6. Have the entire group read the poem again in unison.

Page 13 of the accompanying workbook may be used following this lesson.

Page 29 — Flat Sam

Introduction

identifying objects

Have the children discuss the picture, identifying the names of the objects, since clams may be unfamiliar to some children. Ask how many clams they see, and have them count them going from left to right.

developing vocabulary

It may be necessary to explain that clams are a kind of shellfish that lives in the sand, under the water. Explain that people can dig them out of the sand when the tide goes out. They have two shells that are tightly closed but open up when they are cooked. The inside is good to eat.

Guiding Reading for Comprehension

Have the children study and read the title of the story. Tell them that as they read the story, they will find out who "Flat Sam" is.

reading to answer questions

In the first sentence, have them find the "number" word (*ten*) and the word that tells what kind of clams they were. (*small*) Have them frame the phrase telling where they sat. (*in the sand*) In the second sentence, have them do the same. (*under a log*) For the third sentence, ask how the water felt. (*warm*) Have these three sentences read as a unit. The next sentence tells what clams can do that some other animals cannot do. Have the children find the answer. (*dig in the sand*) Have them read the last sentence aloud.

Pages 30 and 31 — Flat Sam (*continued*)

Guiding Reading for Comprehension

Discuss the picture. Ask, "What is the turtle doing? Why are the clams digging?" Tell the children that the first sentence will tell them what the turtle's name is. Have them find it silently and respond. (*Flat Sam*)

interpreting a picture

The second sentence tells what Flat Sam wanted to do. This is a long sentence, and after a child has answered the question about what Sam wanted to do, have the sentence read aloud. (*to get the clams*) Call the children's attention to the quotation marks in the next part. Review their significance, and then have the class read the first sentence to find out who was talking. (*a clam*) Explain that *ed* added to *call* does not make a second syllable. Direct them to read what the clam said. "What did he tell them to do first?" (*dig*) "Next?" (*get under the sand*) "Where did he tell them to dig?" (*far into the sand*)

reviewing punctuation: quotation marks

This is the first time an exclamation point is emphasized in the text, although the children will probably be familiar with it from their own creative stories and class charts. (See Teacher's Edition, *Book A*, page 35, for suggestions.) Call attention to the mark and ask what it means. Stress that an exclamation point shows excitement. Have the children read the last three sentences aloud as they think the clam would have said them. Emphasize expression to show excitement.

developing punctuation skills: exclamation point

Now discuss page 31 with the children.

Ask the children how Flat Sam went after the clams. (*swam*) Have them point to the word. Ask them to frame the words in the second sentence that tell what the clams did. (*dug and dug*) Call attention to the next sentence, which is a question. Have it read silently, then aloud, for proper inflection.

reading aloud for proper inflection

In the second group of sentences, ask how Flat Sam swam. (*fast*)

Page 32 — Flat Sam (*conclusion*)

Introduction

Here is the conclusion, as shown in the picture: a happy ending for everyone but Flat Sam.

Guiding Reading for Comprehension

checking comprehension

Have the children look at page 32. As the children read the first group of sentences, ask questions similar to those on page 28.

"What noise did the water make?" (*slap, slap*) "Did Flat Sam get the clams?" (*no*) Have the sentence that gives this answer read silently and aloud.

In the last group of sentences ask, "Where were the clams?" (*in the sand*) Direct the children to read both sentences silently; then call on a child to read them aloud.

reading for fluency and continuity

You may prefer to have each thought unit read completely before going on to the next group of sentences, or you may follow the pattern of having the entire page studied and then read aloud. It is not necessary, if this last system is used, to have one child read the entire page, but two or three children can read the page without discussion or interruption, for fluency and continuity.

developing vocabulary of descriptive sounds

Review some of the words which are descriptive of sounds:

1. What sound did the turtle make as he swam in the water? (*slap*)
2. What sound do you make as you walk in puddles? (*slop*)
3. What sound does an apple make when it falls off a tree? (*plop*)
4. What sound do you make when you walk in your daddy's slippers? (*flap*)
5. What sound does the rain make on the window? (*patter*)
6. What sound does a balloon make when it breaks? (*pop*)

As the children respond freely, the teacher should list their responses; or she may write these responses in random order on the board or place flash cards in the pocket chart. As she asks the questions again, the children find the correct "sound" word.

Workbook page 14 follows this lesson.

Enrichment

providing enrichment activities

Poem: Lindsay, Vachel, "The Little Turtle," in *Anthology of Children's Literature,* Houghton Mifflin.

Story: De Huff, Elizabeth W., "The Fox and the Turtle," adapted from *Taytay's Tales,* Harcourt, Brace.

Page 33 — The b sound

phoneme-grapheme relationships

Building Linguistic Skills

The sound of **b** in various positions.

teaching rhythm through nursery rhymes

Introduction

Use one or several nursery rhymes to demonstrate the rhythm, and at the same time, a strong **b** sound: "Baa, Baa, Black Sheep,"

"Bow-wow-wow, Whose Dog Art Thou?" "Little Bo-Peep," or "Bye, Baby Bunting."

Procedure

1. As the children recite these rhymes, exaggerate the position of your lips, and then call attention to their position but the lack of any sound. Put **bow** on the board if you have used that nursery rhyme, or **baa,** etc. Say the word, moving your hand under it so they can see the vowels immediately following the **b.** If you must isolate **b,** remember that no voice sound accompanies **b** except when it is used with a vowel.

introducing the **b** phoneme

This may be learned as a jingle:

"Baby, balloons, button, and bow
All begin with a **b,** you know."

2. Make balloons with the following words for the flannel board. Draw balloons on the board and put the words in them if a flannel board is not available:

bat	big	cob	barn	bump
bad	but	stab	Bob	
bed	rob	ball	crab	
beg	rib	bled	bend	

As the words are read by the children, they can be used in sentences, or in answer to questions such as: "Which word means to steal? Which one is a toy? a home for animals?" (The teacher may use any device to maintain interest.)

developing vocabulary

3. Have the children close their eyes. Remove one word, or erase it. Have the children look at the list and try to guess which word was removed. The one who guesses correctly can remove the next word.

4. Direct the children to shut their eyes. Say a word and have them listen for the initial, medial, or terminal sounds, as: "What is the middle sound in **sob?** What is the last sound in **bled?** What are the first two letter sounds in **crab?"**

recognizing the initial, medial, and terminal sounds of words

5. Encourage the children to think of their own words beginning with **b.** Words with unfamiliar elements, such as in **bottle, button, berry, basket,** and **box** may be listed on the board.

6. Have the children open their books to page 33. Review by saying **balloon,** and then have them read the words on the page.

7. Dictate words to be written on the board. Use the words from the previous list and from the list that is included in the child's text:

providing dictation practice

ban	bond	tub
bar	bun	cab
Ben	bug	cub
best	ebb	hub

bet	garb	stub
bin	rub	bog
bid	brag	boss
blend	brim	bib
blimp	slab	bulb
blot	bass	bald
belt	dab	bull
bit	bag	

Many of these words should be used in sentences, either by the teacher or by the children, to clarify their meanings.

8. Put the words **bed, cab,** and **belt** on the board and have all the **b's** encircled. Include words without **b's** as well, such as **dip** and **put.**

Suggestions for Further Activities

exercises for independent work

1. Have the children find pictures of words that begin with **b** in magazines. Give the children a definite number of pictures to find—four or six.

2. Have them illustrate four (or six or eight) of the **b** words from the textbook.

3. Children enjoy making booklets. Staple folded paper together to make eight pages. Print an initial consonant on each page and have the children either illustrate the consonant with crayon or find pictures of it in magazines.

making booklets

4. Put funny phrases on the board, and have the children make booklets. Here are some examples:

a rat in a hat
a clown on a ball
the dog in a wagon
a cat in a tub

Workbook pages 15, 16, and 17 follow this lesson.

Enrichment

providing enrichment

Poem: Brown, B. C., "Jonathan Bing," in *Anthology of Children's Literature,* Houghton Mifflin.

Page 34 — The terminal sound of le

Building Linguistic Skills

phoneme-grapheme relationships

The two-syllable words resulting from the addition of the **le** phoneme to familiar phoneme-grapheme patterns.

Introduction

Review the sound of *b* briefly, putting *bulb, bump,* and *bog* on the board. Add *bottle* to the list and give a child an opportunity to respond if he is able to.

reviewing the **b** phoneme

Procedure

If no child recognizes the word, pronounce the word and have the class repeat it. Pronounce the others slowly, with an exaggerated sound of the syllables: *little, apple, rattle, sniffle, waffle, rumble, settle.*

introducing the terminal **le** phoneme

Put these words on the board, changing the above order, and have the children read them. Call attention to the double letters after the vowel. If there are two consonants (*rumble*) before **le**, there is no need to double the one before the **le.**

Dictate the following words for spelling:

providing words for dictation

battle
tumble
muffle
grapple
stumble

Use these words in context, either on the board or by making phrase cards:

a little car	a glass bottle
tumble down	the pans rattle
a red apple	stumble up the step
the dogs battle	a ruffle on her dress
a little apple	the waffle is hot
the big car rumbles	settle down
the water ripples	fumble the ball

Duplicating Master No. 8 can be used here.

Page 35 — The Little Sled

Introduction

Discuss the illustration, including the season. Ask, "How do you know it is winter?" (*snow, clothing, etc.*) "How do the boys look?" (*worried*) "Why?" (*The sled is going too fast.*) "What other way can you ride on a sled?" (*lying down, etc.*) "How do the boys steer their sleds?" (*with their feet*)

drawing conclusions from an illustration

Guiding Reading for Comprehension

checking comprehension

Have a child find and read the title. Ask, "Who are the children?" (*Ben and Bob*) Have them find the word in the second sentence which has an **a** changed by an **r**. Call on a child to read the word. (*started*) For the third sentence, ask what the sled started to do, and where it went. (*run, down a hill*) Have the three sentences read aloud.

building suspense to motivate reading

In the second thought unit, have the children find and read the two-syllable word. (*faster*) Ask, "What did Bob and Ben do?" (*held on*) Direct them to read the last line to find out who was talking. (*Bob*) "What did he say?" (*stop the sled*) Have the last unit read aloud. Ask the class what they think happened next; accept all of the suggestions.

Page 36 — The Little Sled (*conclusion*)

Introduction

developing awareness of safety

Discuss the picture for the conclusion. Stress the importance of safety—sliding where it is safe, learning to steer, etc.

Guiding Reading for Comprehension

checking comprehension

Have the children read the first sentence; then ask them what the sled hit. (*a bump*) Ask, "What happened to Bob and Ben?"(*fell from the sled*) Guide the children to read the next three sentences. Ask them if the sled stopped. What words tell them? (*did not*) Ask what happened to the sled. (*ran into the red barn*) In the next sentence ask, "What happened to the sled when it ran into the barn?" (*bent*) "What happened to the barn?" (*dented*) In the last sentence ask, "What happened to Bob and Ben?" (*got wet*) Have the entire page read aloud.

Continue the safety discussion for this story. Encourage free expression of the children's own experiences.

Suggestions for Further Activities

creative drawing

1. Suggest free creative drawing of each child's own experiences in snow. Encourage children to tell the story that their picture illustrates. This can be done orally, as they show their pictures to the class, or again they can be dictated to the teacher who can print or type them.

2. Have the children fill in the missing letter in the following words that you put on the board. Be sure to check to see that they

can read them when they have finished. Letter boxes are useful in this type of exercise.

b__ttle   app____   se____le
l__ttle   waff____   sni____le
r__ffle   st____ble   ri____le

providing independent work

Duplicating Master No. 9 follows this lesson.

Workbook page 18 may be used here. Workbook page 19 is a vocabulary test.

Enrichment

providing poems for enrichment

Poems: Aldis, Dorothy, "Ice," in *The Golden Flute,* Hubbard and Babbitt, Day.

Bush, Joselyn, "The Little Red Sled," in *Arbuthnot Anthology of Children's Literature,* Scott, Foresman.

Miller, Nellie Burget, "The Snow," in *The Golden Flute,* Hubbard and Babbitt, Day.

Turner, Nancy Byrd, "The Best Time of All," in *Anthology of Children's Literature,* Houghton Mifflin.

Wilkins, Alice, "Snow," in *The Golden Flute,* Hubbard and Babbitt, Day.

Wynne, Annette, "Song of the Snowflakes," in *The Golden Flute,* Hubbard and Babbitt, Day.

Page 37 — The initial and terminal k

Building Linguistic Skills

phoneme-grapheme relationships

The sound of **k**, and the rule that usually **k** is used with **i** and **e**, and **c** with **a**, **o**, and **u** to produce this sound.

Introduction

introducing the **k** phoneme

Show either a large mounted picture of a king or the illustration on page 37. Ask who this is. Print the response (*king*) on the board and have the children pronounce it. Explain that there are two letters that have the same sound. (Recall **c** in **cat.**)

Procedure

providing visual discrimination exercises

1. **k** as an initial sound:
   a) Have the children pronounce the following words after you as you write them on the board:

kitten	Kenneth	kiss	kilt
kettle	kitchen	keg	kept

Have the children find and draw a line around the vowels following the **k.** Call attention to the fact that they are all **e** or **i** and explain that **a, o,** and **u** usually follow **c.**

distinguishing between the **c** and **k** graphemes

b) Pronounce the following words and have the children identify the vowel sound. After they have determined the vowel, have them name the initial consonant in each word:

cat	kitten	kitchen	custard
cup	copy	carriage	candy
keg	cuddle	kept	kiss

To make a game of this exercise, draw two trains on the board. Put **c** on the engine of one, and **k** on the engine of the other. After identifying the vowel sound in a word, a child goes to the correct train and puts his initials in it (he is riding on the train). A more permanent device can be made by cutting two trains out of oaktag and making slits for windows. Put the initial consonant on a small piece of oaktag and attach it to the engine with a paper clip. (This makes it possible to use the device for a variety of phonetic situations.) Each child has a small colored "ticket" with his initials on it. When he gives the correct response, he inserts his ticket in a slit, thereby proving he can ride on the train.

playing a game to reinforce the **c** and **k** graphemes

c) Play an active game by having the children stand. Read a list similar to the above to them; the children stoop when they hear a word which begins with **k** (has **i** or **e** as a vowel sound), and stand when they hear the words beginning with **c (a, o, u** vowel sounds).

d) Make a chart on the board and dictate words at random. Have the children put them in the proper column, either under **c** or **k.**

cat	kit	kitten
cup	cot	cat
kill	cub	keg
cost	kilt	cob
cast	kept	kiss

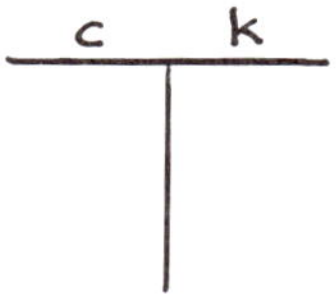

recognizing **k** in a terminal position

2. **k** as a terminal consonant after **s, l,** and **r:**
   a) Say **milk** and have someone tell where he hears the **k** sound. Call on a child to write it on the board. Follow with **silk, task, mask, risk,** and **dark.**
   b) Have the children read the words on page 37 that have **k** at the beginning and that have **k** following a consonant other than **c.**
3. Do an exercise similar to (d) in exercise 1 above, adding **k** as a terminal sound:

c	k	-k

Use the same list, but include *mask, task, risk, silk, milk, dark, park,* and *mark.*

Workbook page 20 follows this lesson.
Duplicating Master No. 10 can be used here.

providing exercises for independent work

Page 38 — A poem: Mitten, mitten

Introduction

This poem creates a picture of a little kitten on a mat.

Procedure

1. Have the children read the poem silently.
2. Ask for the name of the animal—cat or kitten. Ask what the children think the kitten looks like. Bring out, if the children do not, that he has paws like mittens and is wearing a mitten on one paw.
3. Ask for two pairs of rhyming words. (*kitten, mitten; cat, mat*)
4. Have the children read the poem in unison; then two or three may read it to the group for enjoyment.

Workbook page 21 follows this lesson.

checking comprehension

locating rhyming words

Page 39 — Words ending with ck

Building Linguistic Skills

The rule that usually the **ck** phoneme follows a short vowel that has no other consonant following it.

phoneme-grapheme relationships

Introduction

Direct the children's attention to the picture of the **sock.** Ask what the last sound is. (*k*) Do they hear any sound after the vowel before the **k** as they do in **milk** or **dark?** (*no*) Explain that when the **k** sound follows the vowel and comes at the end of a word, we use **ck** for the sound. Have the children read the **ck** words in the text.

introducing the **ck** graphemic pattern

Procedure

distinguishing between **k** and **ck** graphemic patterns

1. Pronounce a word from the list in the book and have the children listen to decide whether there is another sound between the vowel and the **k** sound.

2. Put the word **milk** on the board and call attention to the **k** after **l** in **milk** and the **ck** after **a** in **sack**, etc. This rule must be repeated many times for mastery. Use the list on page 39.

3. Put **k** and **ck** on the board, or have the children fold writing paper and put **k** and **ck** at the top:

k	**ck**

Dictate **mask, tick, truck, ask, lock, peck, dark,** and have the children write them under the correct headings. Use also:

desk	task	rack	park
risk	pick	milk	luck
pack	dusk	duck	lark
dock	silk	rock	sock

Suggestions for Further Activities

providing further activities for discrimination

1. For more difficult experiences, put on the board lines such as "A tisket, a tasket, a little yellow basket," "Lucy Locket lost her pocket," and "Five, six, pick up sticks." Have the children find the **k** sounds, read the words, and develop the sentences. Nursery rhymes can then be said in unison or by individuals.

exercises for independent work

2. Have the children complete words either from the board or on a duplicated paper. Give them the initial sound, example:

sil___, mas___, la___, etc.

3. Have the children add **ck** to the following initial sounds and illustrate them.

ro_____	ta_____	ne_____	ki_____
so_____	du_____	si_____	sti_____

Duplicating Master No. 11 gives additional practice with the **ck** digraph and may be used following this lesson.

Page 40 — A poem: A camel had an Arab on his back

Introduction

Discuss the illustration with the children, helping them to identify the Arab, and the camel, too, if necessary. Ask how the children think it feels to ride on a camel.

interpreting the story illustration

Procedure

1. Have the children read the poem silently to answer the above question.
2. Ask if there are any difficult words. Develop these through linguistic clues if necessary.
3. Read the poem with the children, stressing the rhythm and the bumpy feeling.
4. If you wish, have two groups read it, the first reading the first three lines and the last, the second group, supplying the fourth sentence. Let them all read the last line together. Do not make this a laborious task. It should be fun. If necessary, read a line to the group to emphasize the rhythm.

improving sense of rhyme and rhythm

Workbook page 22 follows this lesson.

Page 41 — Words ending in nk

Building Linguistic Skills

phoneme-grapheme relationships

The terminal blend **nk.**

Introduction

Call attention to the illustration. Have the children say the words **pink, drink** (illustration) after you, prolonging the terminal sound. Ask if they ever had a pink drink—a pink soda. Allow time for discussion of personal experiences.

introducing the terminal **nk** phonemic pattern

Procedure

building auditory discrimination of **ck** and **nk** phonemic patterns

1. Have the children repeat after you—**bank, ink, tank, sunk.** Emphasize in your pronunciation the difference of the **n** when followed by **k.** Point out that the sound is rather nasal in quality, coming through the nose. Say paired words, such as **sink** and **sick, bank** and **back,** emphasizing the **nk.** Now say pairs, and ask which (first or second) had the **nk** ending. Here are some possibilities:

tack - tank	sink - sick	pink - pick
hank - hack	tick - ink	sank - sack
spank - stack	wick - wink	rank - rack

enriching vocabulary

2. Have the children read the words in the book. As each word is read, ask a child to use it in a sentence. Encourage them to use all the meanings of such words as: **tank**—an army tank, an oil tank, a fish tank; **sink**—the kitchen sink, to sink; **bank**—to put in a bank, a savings bank, a river bank. Time spent on enriching a child's vocabulary is never wasted. It may be well to note here that we do not teach the meaning of a word only as it is to be used in the story. Therefore, it is not necessary to drill on the word as it is to be found in context. As the phoneme-grapheme patterns are presented and analyzed, the word meanings are developed.

exercises for dictation

3. Dictate some of the words from page 41, using them in phrases or sentences, and have the children write them. The entire group may write them on paper while individual children write the words on the board. Here are some suggested sentences and words for this exercise.

bank: "I put my money in the bank." **bank**
sink: "Did the boat sink?" **sink**
link: "Each part of a chain is a link." **link**
ink: "We use ink in pens." **ink**
sank: "The rock sank to the bottom of the lake." **sank**
drink: "Did you drink your milk?" **drink**
rink: "We skate at the rink." **rink**
tank: "We have a tank for hot water in the basement." **tank**
mink: "A mink is a small animal whose fur is very valuable." **mink**
wink: "Let me see you wink." **wink**

Suggestions for Further Activities

1. Give the children a duplicated sheet with pictures (Duplicating Master No. 12). Have them complete the words under each picture. For example:

2. Put the following sentences on a duplicated sheet or use Duplicating Master No. 13, and have the children draw a line around the correct word and put the word on the line.

further exercises for discrimination of terminal blends

Ann's drink is ________.
pink pick

The rock ________ in the water.
sank sack

The ________ wall is red.
brink brick

Put ________ in the pen.
silk ink

Workbook page 23 follows this lesson.

Pages 42 and 43 — The Black Cow

Introduction

In discussing the picture, bring out that this is the country. Point out how it differs from the city. This is an excellent opportunity to enrich the children's knowledge of both the city and the country. Ask the children where they get their milk. Many will have no understanding beyond the milkman who delivers the milk each morning, or the local grocery store. Bring out other differences

enriching class knowledge of city and country

taking field trip or using films related to the story

—the presence of trees, fields, few houses with much land, as contrasted with apartment houses and playgrounds, etc. It would be worthwhile here to have good mounted illustrations of skyscrapers or city traffic, as well as pictures of farms, country roads, etc.

The ideal would be a field trip to a local farm or dairy where the children can actually see cows—see them being cared for and milked. If this is an impossibility, as it is for many areas today, there are several good films available, such as "Uncle Jim's Dairy Farm," loaned by the National Dairy Council, and others as suggested on page 101 of this Teacher's Edition.

developing understanding of milk processing

Sets of posters are available from the National Dairy Council that explain the steps from the time the cow is milked, through the taking of the milk to the local milk depot, where most farmers take their milk, then transporting the milk via tank train or tank truck to the city where it is homogenized, pasteurized, bottled, etc., at the milk plant, and lastly, delivered by truck to homes and stores.

Stress the importance of cleanliness of the cow, and everything that comes in contact with the milk.

Guiding Reading for Comprehension

reading the title to learn about the story

From the previous discussion of the picture, the title could include the farm, the boy, the cat, or the cow. Have the children read the title to find out what the story is about. (*the black cow*) Continue the silent reading to find out the name of the boy, (*Bob*) the new word in the second line (*kept*), what Bob does to the cow, (*rubs her back and neck*) and how the cow feels toward Bob. (*will not harm*) Follow with reading aloud. Ask the children why they think the cat is there.

making inferences from pictures

From the picture, have the children identify what Bob is doing. Do they think this is a big farm or a little one? (*little—one cow, milked by hand; a large farm would have many cows milked by machines*) Now have them tell why the cat is there. Ask what the cat wants. (*milk*) Say, "Yes, it wants *a drink of milk.*" Put the phrase on the board, moving your hand under it as you reread it, and then have a child read it. Have another child frame **of.** Guide them to find **of** on page 43.

Direct the children to read the first two sentences, and then ask, "What does Bob want? (*to get milk*) What can Bob do?" (*can milk*) Have both sentences read aloud.

checking comprehension

Tell the children that the next sentence gives the cat's name, and also its color. Have the children find these two words. (*Tab, tan*) Ask what the cat does. Be sure they read the second sentence to find out. (*begs*) Direct the children to read the last sentence silently before reading the three sentences together. The last three sentences can be read by three children, and then by one child. The page can be reread by two children, or the entire story (two pages) can be reread aloud by several children.

Discuss further what kind of animal a cow is. (*farm animal rather than a zoo animal or pet*) Then discuss what kind of animal a cat is. (*pet, or farm animal*) How does the cat help the farmer? (*catches mice in the barn*)

Suggestions for Further Activities

learning about categorizing animals

1. This lesson should be used to enrich the child's background, either through further study of country life, or through categorizing animals as zoo animals, pets, wild animals, or farm animals. A series of lessons can include the habits of each type, as well as recognition of familiar animals and their characteristics. Some of the categories might include animals with similar coverings: fur, hair, feathers, scales, shells, etc.; or animals with similar methods of moving: four legs, two legs and wings, six legs, many legs, no legs, fins, etc.; or homes: nest, burrow, hole in tree, cave.

exercises for independent work

2. Many independent activities can be suggested, such as, making scrapbooks of animals by categories, or experience charts. Some examples are:

I am an elephant.
I am very big.
I have a long trunk to help lift big logs.

The farmer has horses and cows.
The cows give us milk.
The horses help pull the farm wagon.

using riddles to develop vocabulary

3. The following riddles can be used orally:

I am a small animal.
I say, "Quack, quack."
I am a good swimmer.
What animal am I? (*a duck*)

I live in a nest.—I am a _____. (*bird*)
I live in a barn.—I begin with **c.** (*cow*)
I lay eggs.—I begin with **h.** (*hen*)

4. Have the children complete words to make the names of farm animals:

c__w	pi__
ca__	__en
d__g	d__ck

Use Duplicating Master No. 14 to make scrapbooks.
Workbook pages 24, 25, and 26 follow this lesson.

Enrichment

Animal Tale: "The Little Red Hen and the Grain of Wheat," in Hutchinson's *Chimney Corner Stories,* Putnam's.

Poems: Mitchell, Lucy Sprague, "The Farmer Tries to Sleep," in *Here and Now Story Book,* Dutton.
Stevenson, R. L., "The Cow," in *A Child's Garden of Verses,* Oxford.

providing stories for enrichment

Stories: Beatty, John Y., *Story Pictures of Farm Animals,* Beckley Cardy.
Brown, Margaret Wise, *Baby Animals,* Random.
Brown, Margaret Wise, *Country Noisy Book,* Scott, Foresman.
Hader, Berta and Elmer, *Cock-a-Doodle Doo,* Macmillan.
Hader, Berta and Elmer, *Farmer in the Dell,* Macmillan.
Lenski, Lois, *The Little Farm,* Oxford.
Meeks, Esther K., *Friendly Farm Animals,* Follett.
Mitchell, Lucy Sprague, "Eben's Cows," and "The Milk's Journey," in *Here and Now Story Book,* Dutton.

Pages 44 and 45 — Introduction of the signal e

Building Linguistic Skills

phoneme-grapheme relationships

A careful and thorough presentation of the signal **e** results in a child's being able to read many new words. The following suggested introduction should be adapted to meet the class situation.

Introduction

Explain that many children in the class are not called by their real names, but by their "nicknames," or short names. Robert's real name is Robert, but his friends and his family call him "Bobby" or "Bob," which is a short name. Sue's real name is Susan, which is her long name, but we often call her "Sue." Tom's real name is Thomas, and Ned's is Edward. So most of us have a long way of saying our names, but we also have a short way that we use very often. So it is with the vowel sounds.

introducing short and long **a**

At this point, either point to **a** in the alphabet or write **a** on the board. Ask the children for the name of this letter (they are entirely familiar with the alphabet by now). Say, "Yes, that **a** (letter name) is the real name, like our real names; so we call it the *long* sound of the letter. Ask for the sound of **a** they have heard in **can.** Explain that this is like our short names. It is still a sound of **a,** but does not say its real name, so we call it a *short* sound of **a.** Therefore, when **a** says its own name, we call it *long;* when it says **a,** we call it *short.*

Procedure

1. Explain that there are several ways to tell when the **a** is long. Today we will learn the easiest way. Take the flash card **can** (or print it on the board). Have a child read the word. Add **e,** using a small card, or add it to the word on the board. Call their attention to what has been added to **can.** Explain that we call this a "signal **e"** because it signals the sound represented by the other vowel in monosyllabic words. The **e** does not represent a sound itself. It is silent. It serves as a signal that the other vowel usually changes from a short sound to a long sound. Use flash cards **mat, rat, man, tam,** and **hat,** following the same procedure.

presenting the long **a** phoneme

changing short **a** to long **a** with signal **e**

2. Dictate one of the above words and have a child write it on the board. Then call on a second child to change it. For example, if the first child puts **fat** on the board, a second child will change it to **fate.** Don't have the second child print the entire word, but merely add the **e** to the original word.

3. Call attention to the first eight words on page 44; discuss them with the children. Ask what kind of vowel they hear in **can, cane,** etc., so that they will not only change the words and read them correctly, but will also become completely familiar with the terms "short" and "long" in this situation.

providing exercises in auditory discrimination

4. Now dictate words at random, and the children must discern whether there is a long or short vowel, and therefore whether they must remember the **e.**

words for dictation practice

Here is a suggested list:

man	stab	bale	fade
mane	state	bat	cast
game	late	same	hate
tame	lap	ram	drab
pan	snap	rate	date
pane	mare	came	had

Several children can be involved simultaneously if you have a group at the board and give each child a different word to print. This also eliminates any possibility of copying.

5. Have the children open their books again and look at page 45. In changing **car** to **care,** call the children's attention to the fact that the "signal **e"** can even change the vowel in the **ar** sound. They can forget that **a** and **r** are together when they see the "signal **e."** Continue to read the words with **ar** in the book. This **a** varies greatly in sound from place to place. It is not a long **a** in most locations.

changing the vowel in **ar** to long **a** with signal **e**

Suggestions for Further Activities

Put the following words on the board, have the children add **e** and illustrate the resulting word. As you give this assignment, give developing vocabulary

the children an opportunity to discover the resulting word and discuss its meaning. For example, the word **mate** suggests socks that go together, or shoes that go together. A **mare** may not be within the child's understanding vocabulary.

can___	at___	pan___
mat___	cap___	mar___

Page 46 — Further experience with long a words

Procedure

1. The additional words on page 46 can be used for rapid drill around the class, or in any way that the teacher chooses. It is important also that the teacher call attention to the **k** in **make, sake,** etc. After a long vowel, only the **k** is used. Here is an excellent opportunity for developing vocabulary; have a child read a word, and then use it in a sentence. You may also put a sentence on the board, have the children read it silently (allowing time for silent study here is essential), and then call on a child to read it orally. Have the child, or another child, locate the "signal **e**," underline the word, and pronounce it. (*Note*: **sail, tail, hair,** and **bear** are not used for these exercises.)

Here are a few suggestions:

teaching long **a** words

Tell the **tale** of Rags and Tags. (Here you explain the difference in meaning between **tale** and **tail.**)

The men shot up a **flare.** (Again, explanation of the meaning is important.)

This rug was on **sale.** (If a child gives the meaning of **sail,** clarify it; otherwise, it is not necessary to refer to **sail.**)

The **hare** can hop and run fast. (different from **hair**)

The sun tans **bare** legs and backs. (different from **bear**)

The **mare** has a black mane.

2. Select from the flash cards the following words: **can, at, rat, cap, mat, fat, car, star, spar,** and **far.** Put them with the long **a** words for rapid discriminatory drill.

3. Select words from the list for the children to write on the board. Call on as many children as board space will permit, and give each child his own word to write. Avoid having all the children write the same word.

Suggestions for Further Activities

making fine auditory discriminations

1. After these words have been dictated for spelling and the children have a good basic understanding, a more difficult dictation lesson would include such words as **ball, saw, pan, black,** and **far,** as well as the long **a** words. Give the children an opportunity to recall other linguistic rules and make fine discriminations.

exercises for independent work

2. List these words on the board. For independent work, have the children add **e**, read, and illustrate the new words.

can	mar	tam	Sal
cap	man	at	Sam

3. Active games can be played with flash cards. Let one child hold a flash card so that all can see it; call on a child to read it. Call another child (a signal) with **e** card to stand beside the first child and add his **e** to the word. Have the child read—**cane.**

These words can be used:

can	at	rat	cap	par	hat	fad
mat	fat	gap	pan	ball	war	gall
car	bar	bass	slat	far	Sam	stall
mar	star	tall	pal	tam	man	

Note: In cases where the word ends in **ll** or **ss,** direct the child with the **e** to cover the final **l** or **s.**

Duplicating Master No. 15 can be used here.

Workbook page 27 follows this lesson.

Page 47 — Black Mane and Tim

Introduction

continuing to learn about farm life

This story follows a farm theme and gives an additional opportunity for the children to learn about life on a farm. The illustration should be used as a basis for such a discussion. Ask such questions as, "What animals do you see? (*rabbit, horse*) What is another name for rabbit? (*hare*) Where are these animals? (*on a farm*) Who lives in the building? (*animals*) What kind of building is it? (*barn*) Why do they have a fence?" (*to hold animals*) These questions will recall previous facts about the farm.

Guiding Reading for Comprehension

checking comprehension

Have the children study the title, and then have one child read it aloud. Ask who "Black Mane" is and why the horse is so named. (*black as slate*) Ask who Tim must be. (*hare*) Have the children read silently to find out what kind of horse Black Mane is. (*pet mare*) At this point, if the word **mare** has not been discussed in a previous lesson, it will be necessary either to find out if the children know the meaning of the word, or to explain that a mare is a female (mother) horse. Have the children read the second line to find the word that tells how black her mane is. Call on a child to describe Black Mane in his own words. Then have another child read the two lines orally.

making inferences from the story

Tell the children that the next line describes Tim. Have them find the words that describe (use this term) him or tell what he looks like. (*small, brown*) The last line tells what they did together. (*ate the grass*) Have the entire page read orally. Before turning the page, ask if the children think Black Mane and Tim are friends.

Page 48 — Black Mane and Tim (*continued*)

Introduction

interpreting picture clues

In presenting this picture, emphasize that very few snakes are harmful. The hare is small and frightened.

Guiding Reading for Comprehension

drawing conclusions

Have the class point to the word **snake.** How many times can they find it on the page? (3) "How did the snake look at Tim?" (*stare*) "What words describe the snake?" (*big, black*) Have the page read orally. Ask the children what they think will happen next. Suggest a happy ending if they tend toward only unhappy conclusions.

The teacher must use her own judgment on the number of questions she should ask during the guided reading part of the lesson. For an average group or better, too many questions will slow the lesson down. Questions are included here to meet the teacher's needs, but she is not expected to use all of them with every group.

oral reading for expression

With most groups, this page can be used as a single unit. Have the children read the page, and then ask, "How did Tim get Black Mane to run fast?" (*He told her to.*) Have the page read aloud. Work for expression, particularly in quotations.

Page 49 — Black Mane and Tim (*conclusion*)

Guiding Reading for Comprehension

checking comprehension

Have the first three sentences read to find out how tall the gate was. (*as tall as the mare*) After the children have read and responded to the thought question, ask what Black Mane asked Tim to do. (*help*) This procedure gives a question before the children read: they are reading to find out. Then, after they have finished reading, ask another question to check their comprehension.

reviewing pronunciations of the *ed* suffix

The next three sentences present the second situation where the *ed* added to the base word does not result in a two-syllable word. For the sake of the story, it is necessary to include it here. Have the children read the fourth line silently. Then call on a child to read it aloud. Through common usage, he will probably read it correctly. However, if he does not, correct him by saying, "That *is* how it looks, because that is the way it is spelled, but how do we say it?" Some child in the group will undoubtedly pronounce it correctly. If no one knows, it will be necessary to tell them.

Have the children read the next sentence silently; then orally. Have them read the last sentence to find out how the story ends. Call on a child to read the last three sentences for continuity.

developing reasons for liking the story

Ask the children if they liked the story. If so, try to find out why. Is it because it is an animal story, or do they like stories about horses, or is it the plot—the snake trying to get the rabbit, and the latter being rescued? Such a discussion can also help children to understand that friends working together can accomplish much. Ask, "Did the hare need the horse's help?" (*yes*) "Did the horse need the hare's help?" (*yes*) Any lesson or moral from this story should be built around this point.

providing creative writing experiences

Here is another natural point from which to build creative stories. Show pictures of animals, or give each child a picture, and have him create his own story.

Duplicating Master No. 16 follows this lesson.

Workbook page 28 follows this lesson.

Enrichment

stories of horses and rabbits for enrichment

Beim, Lorraine and Jerrold, *Two Is a Team,* Harcourt. (An excellent book to bring out this same point—working together is the only way.)

Stories of Horses: Anderson, C. W., *Billy and Blaze,* Macmillan.
Gall, Alice Crew and Crew, Fleming, "The Song of the Little Donkey," in *Told Under the Magic Umbrella,* Macmillan.

Stories of Rabbits: Aesop, "The Hare and the Tortoise," in *Anthology of Children's Literature,* Houghton Mifflin.

Bailey, Carolyn Sherwin, *The Rabbit Who Wanted Red Wings,* Platt and Munk.

Young, Martha, "How Mr. Rabbit got a Good Dinner," and "The Dyeing of Mr. Rabbit," in Bailey, *Merry Tales for Children,* Platt and Munk.

Page 50 — The long sound of e and ee

been

Building Linguistic Skills

phoneme-grapheme relationships

Continuation of long vowel sounds, including terminal **e** and the **ee** digraph.

Introduction

Review the story of our long names and our short names. Put a child's name (from the class) on the board in a sentence:

Stan can run.

teaching the pronoun *he*

Have a child read it. Under it write:

He can run fast.

Ask the children what word was used instead of repeating *Stan.* (*He*)

Procedure

introducing the long **e** phoneme

1. Have a child read the sentence; then have another underline **He.** Repeat **He** and ask what sound they hear. (*long e*) Change **He** to **We** and have the sentence read.

2. Put **me** on the board and have it read, and then write **Pete** (calling attention to the signal **e**) and **here.**

providing exercises in auditory discrimination of long **e**

3. Put **be** on the board, and use it in a sentence orally; explain that there are other ways of showing a long **e.** When two vowels come together, we *usually* hear the long sound of the first one; the other is silent. This is called a vowel digraph. Add **e** to **be** and have a child draw a line around the double **e's.** Have it read as a long **e.** Use it in a sentence.

4. Direct the children to turn to page 50. Discuss the illustration. As the children pronounce **bee,** put the word on the board and

have them find the vowels. Teach them that **e** or **ee** can make the long **e** sound.

5. Have the children read the words at the bottom of the page. Use many of these words in sentences to clarify the meanings. For instance, **steel** should be used correctly and not confused with **steal;** and **deer** should not be confused with **dear.**

6. Use **been** in a sentence: *He has been here for a week.* Have the children mark all the long **e's,** and read the sentence orally. Notice the pronunciation of **been** and explain that it is a special word which most people pronounce **bin.** Some people say **bēēn.**

reviewing long and short sounds of **a** and **e**

7. Put other phrases or sentences on the board, reviewing the long and short **a** and **e.** Have the children read the sentence, then underline and pronounce the long and short vowel words.

a) Pete has seen his pet.
b) Did Ann take her hat?
c) We will rake the grass.
d) He has a bat and ball to trade.
e) We need a bed for Sam.
f) The deer ran up the steep hill.
g) Make a cake for Ann.
h) The mare is for sale.

Suggestions for Further Activities

providing exercises for independent work

1. Activity 7 in the preceding section can be set up for independent work. Directions should be at the top of the paper, followed by sentences similar to those used in step 7. The children could be directed to mark words with long **e** with a green crayon, and words having long **a** with a red crayon. Duplicating Master No. 17 has a similar exercise.

2. Make a duplicated sheet with vowels missing from words. The children identify the words from the pictures and fill in the missing vowels. Duplicating Master No. 18 is a similar exercise.

3. Have the children find words with **ee** on pages torn from newspapers or magazines. The children circle words and read those they can recognize.

Workbook page 29 follows this lesson.

Enrichment

providing enrichment

The following poem can be taught.

In the heart of a seed, buried deep, so deep,
A dear little plant lay fast asleep.

Write the poem on a piece of oaktag and have the children frame the words with **ee** and read them.

Page 51 — Red Deer

Introduction

drawing story parallels

Discuss details of the picture. The deer eating the beets can be compared to Peter Rabbit in Mr. McGregor's garden. Bring out the childish fun in the Peter Rabbit story, and draw parallels.

Guiding Reading for Comprehension

introducing two-line sentences

developing oral reading skills

Read the title to learn the deer's name. (*Red Deer*) These stories in which the animals have names are more like the old Thornton Burgess favorites, or *Mother West Wind Stories*. The attitude of the teacher should be to maintain the tenor of such stories. Direct the children to read the first three sentences. Call their attention to a sentence that goes from one line to another. The sentence starts with a capital and ends with a period. After silent reading, ask what kind of farm it was. (*beet farm*) What word describes the deer? (*Red*) Have a child read the two-line sentence again. Have a child read the last three sentences. Be sure the last sentence is read without hesitation.

Page 52 — Red Deer (*continued*)

Guiding Reading for Comprehension

Call the children's attention to the next long sentence. This tells why the farmer has a stick. After silent reading, have the entire sentence read orally. Several children may read it for fluency. Have the children read the next two sentences silently, and then orally. Complete the page in this way.

Page 53 — Red Deer (*conclusion*)

Guiding Reading for Comprehension

locating answers to questions

There are several two-line sentences on this page. Give the children an opportunity to read these sentences silently before reading the page orally. Ask questions to review the story after they read silently. "What could the farmer see?" Say, "Put your finger on the word that tells the answer." (*antlers*) "How did Red Deer get away? Put your finger on the word that tells what Red Deer did." (*swam*) "Did the farmer hit Red Deer?" (*no*) "Will Red Deer return to the farm?" (*no*) "Where will he get his food?" (*forest*) Have the page read in thought units by several children.

Discuss Red Deer and what he eats in the forest, his speed in swimming and running, his slim legs and great antlers. Bring out how nature has equipped Red Deer to protect himself.

A natural conclusion to this story would be a discussion of taking care of animals. The children will be familiar with taking care of pets, but here you may bring out how we take care of animals in the forest. Also discuss how these animals find ways to protect themselves. Bring out the fact that the deer hid because it was afraid. Animals are often afraid of people.

Duplicating Master No. 19 can be used as a comprehension check for the story.

Enrichment

providing enrichment stories

Jackson, Kathryn and Byron, *Big Farmer Big and Little Farmer Little,* Simon.

Lenski, Lois, *The Little Farm,* Oxford.

Page 54 — Vowel digraph ea

Building Linguistic Skills

phoneme-grapheme relationships

Continuation of long **e** sound—**ea**

Introduction

introducing homophones

Review the vowel digraph rule, recalling that when two vowels come together we usually hear the long sound of the first vowel. Put **see** on the board, then—*He can see me.* Under **see,** put **sea.** *The sea is big.* Explain that **see** and **sea** sound the same but have different meanings. Have a child read the second sentence, and then clarify the meaning, if necessary.

Procedure

1. After you have put the following list of words on the board, have one child draw a line around the vowel digraphs in each. Then have another pronounce the first word, and another repeat the vowel sound he hears, telling whether it is long or short.

feet	feat
meet	meat
peek	peak
beet	beat

Use the words in sentences to show their meanings.

developing vocabulary

2. Use the books to read many words containing long **ea.** Have the children find the words in answer to such directions as those listed below:

Find the name of an animal who swims. (*seal*)
Find another name for the ocean. (*sea*)
Find the name of a vegetable. (*bean* or *pea*)
Find something to eat. (*meat*)
Find a part of our body. (*ear*)
Find a word that tells how we should keep our room and our desk. (*neat*)
Find what we sit on. (*seat*)
Find a word we use to be polite. (*please*)
Find what Santa Claus has. (*beard*)
Find something on a tree. (*leaf*)
Find something we get from the sun. (*heat*)
Find another word for jump. (*leap*)
Find what we are learning to do. (*read*)

further homophone discrimination activities

3. Use flash cards with the words from page 54 to drill the class on all the words. Two teams may be formed. Keep score of the right responses to see who wins. Many uses of flash cards may be found. They may be put in the card holder and questions like those included above used. Individuals may be called on, and then two children can be chosen. The question (or word) is given and the two will race to see who can find it first.

4. A word may be shown on the flash card and the children called on to put a rhyming word on the board.

Suggestions for Further Activities

1. Correlate with writing by having the children copy the following list and mark the vowels as *long* or *short*: exercises for independent work

here	me
bed	meat
seam	net
see	east
fell	end
feat	eat

2. Have the children illustrate their own animal booklets. Use Duplicating Master No. 20. making animal booklets

a black seal	a bumble bee	a little hare
a brown deer	a green snake	a tame mare
a dear little cat	a beast of the forest	

3. Give the children a sheet like the following. Have them complete the words. Tell them to use pages 50 and 54 for reference.

___ee___	___ea___
___ee___	___ea___
___ee___	___ea___
___ee___	___ea___
___ee___	___ea___

4. Give the children these simple riddles. The answers will be found on page 54. Have them write the correct answer on the lines. using riddles to develop vocabulary

It is deep.
It is big.
It is wet.
It is the s___. (*sea*)

It can be a cat.
It can be a dog.
It can be a deer in the forest.
It is a b_____. (*beast*)

It falls from a tree.
It is brown in winter.
It can be red and yellow.
It is a l_____. (*leaf*)

It is in a cup.
It is hot.
We drink it.
It is t___. (*tea*)

Duplicating Master No. 21 duplicates these riddles. Duplicating Master No. 22 also follows this lesson.

Note: Many of these suggested activities will be needed only for the slower learners.

Workbook page 30 can be used here or after page 57.

Enrichment

Story: Asbjornsen, P. C., "The Lad Who Went to the North Wind," in *Anthology of Children's Literature,* Houghton Mifflin.
Hoff, Syd, *Sammy, the Seal,* Harper.

providing enrichment activities

Poem: Stevenson, R. L., "At the Seaside," in *A Child's Garden of Verses,* Oxford.

Page 55 — Don and Nell Dig Clams

using pictures to develop story background

Introduction

The scene in this illustration may be completely unfamiliar to many children. It may be necessary for the teacher to repeat that clams are shellfish and that they are dug out of the mud under the water. Allow the children to ask questions.

checking comprehension

Guiding Reading for Comprehension

Have the title read to discover whom the story is about and what they are doing. Direct the children to read the first two sentences to find out where this story takes place. (*at the sea*) After the class has read this thought unit, ask why Nell wanted clams. (*to eat*)

The second thought unit describes what the children need. (*a bucket and a rake*) After finding the names of the tools, have each sentence read orally. Strive for fluency with two-line sentences.

Page 56 — Don and Nell Dig Clams (*continued*)

Special Word I

I

introducing the pronoun *I*

As the long **i** sound has not yet been introduced, the word **I** is treated as a special word. It will be included with the long **i** group, but is needed at this time in the story. It should be enough to call the attention of the group to the **I** at the bottom of the page. When a child has identified it by letter name, tell him that this is the word we use when speaking of ourselves. Have the children find **I** in the story, and call on a child to read the sentence aloud.

reading to answer questions

Guiding Reading for Comprehension

Ask, "Did the children get any clams?" (*yes*) How will they cook them?" (*steam*) Allow time for silent reading to find the answers. "In order to get steam, what must the children do?" (*heat water*)

"Who will heat the water?" (*Nell*) Follow the silent reading with oral reading. Call attention to the one-syllable pronunciation of *steamed.*

Page 57 — Don and Nell Dig Clams (*conclusion*)

Introduction

enjoying the picture

Allow time for enjoyment of the picture.

Guiding Reading for Comprehension

Ask, "Who is talking first? What did she say?" (*Nell, Please pass me a clam.*) Have the words in the quotations read orally. Ask what the children did next, and have the words read orally. (*ate clams*)

In the next thought unit, ask how many clams each child ate. (*Nell, 10; Don, 15*)

Finally, ask how they felt after they had eaten. (*full*) Have the entire page read orally.

relating personal experiences to the story

As this may be a new experience for many children, the story can be reread for pleasure. Also, children can be encouraged to talk about their own experiences at the beach or at a lake.

Suggestions for Further Activities

1. Have the children illustrate their own experiences at the beach, or camping, etc.

creative writing exercise

2. Encourage creative writing at every opportunity. Here the children may compose two- or three-sentence stories to accompany their pictures. These stories can be written by the children, with the teacher assisting with words that the children cannot spell.

3. If a story seems difficult for any child at this time, try having him make up only a title to accompany his picture. He will begin to grasp the difference between a sentence and a title.

Workbook page 31 follows this lesson.

Duplicating Master No. 23 can be used here.

Enrichment

providing enrichment activities

Story: McCloskey, Robert, *One Morning in Maine,* Viking.

Poems: Field, Rachel, "I'd Like to Be a Lighthouse," in *Taxis and Toadstools,* Doubleday.

Milne, A. A., "Sand-Between-the-Toes," in *When We Were Very Young,* Dutton.

Page 58 — Vowel digraph ai

phoneme-grapheme relationships

Building Linguistic Skills

Introduction of **ai** digraph.

Introduction

reviewing long vowel rules

Review the rule for the signal **e** that changes the short **a** to a long **a.** Ask whether there is another way a long vowel sound may be spelled. (*When two vowels come together, usually the long sound of the first vowel is heard.*)

Procedure

introducing the **ai** digraph

1. Put **ai** on the board. Ask for the name of the first letter. Recall that the name of the letter is the long sound. Change **ai** to **rain** and have the children read it. Change it to **train, brain, sprain.** Have a child draw a line around the digraph in each word and read the word.

2. Dictate the following words, having several children at the board simultaneously, and giving each a different word. (This technique keeps the group involved and alert.)

aim	air	hair	pair
tail	sail	pail	mail
paid	raid	maid	braid
bait	wait	waist	grain

locating the **ai** digraph

3. Have the children read the following sentences as you put them on the board:

Paint the barn red.
The mailman has a letter.
Her hair is in a braid.
The water went down the drain.
The train runs fast.
We can sail in the wind.
Dig a pail of sand.
Can he hammer a nail?

As each sentence is read, call on a child to mark the long **a.**

4. Put **tale** and **tail** on the board and ask a child to use **tale** in a sentence. If this seems difficult, provide the sentence—for exam-

ple, "I like 'The Tale of Peter Rabbit.' "—and explain the meaning of **tale.** Move on to **tail** and ask the children to use this word in a sentence. (*Peter Rabbit has a fluffy tail.*) This is not so difficult for them. Explain that there are many words which sound like other words but mean something different and are spelled differently. Now put **sale** and **sail** under **tale** and **tail** on the board and develop the meanings in the same way. Add **hare** and **hair, bare** and **bear,** and **plane** and **plain** and follow the same procedure, using each in a simple sentence.

developing vocabulary: homophones

5. Direct the children to turn to page 58. Have each one study the list, choose a word, use it in a sentence orally, and write it on the board. Each child may call on another child to read a word and use it.

6. After most of the words have been read, those which were not chosen may be listed on the board by the teacher and read by the children. The teacher may find it necessary to explain some meanings.

7. Direct the children to the irregular word **again** at the bottom of the page. Use it in a sentence orally, and call on a child to tell which of the words in the sentence he thinks is the word **again.** Here is a suggested sentence: *It is raining again.* Point out that **again** is sometimes pronounced with a long **a** sound. Call on several children to use **again** in a sentence.

introducing the irregular word *again*

8. Put the flash card for **again** with the group to be used for **ai.** Direct the children to put their hands up when they see it. Expose the cards quickly. Do not have the children read them, but have them raise their hands quickly when they see **again.** Repeat this procedure several times, changing the position of the card each time.

9. Have a short review of words with flash cards. When the children are familiar with these words to the point of rapid recognition, mix cards with **ee** and **ea** words for further word mastery.

Suggestions for Further Activities

independen exercises reviewing **ai, ea, ee**

1. Put a list of words on the board for the children to read, illustrate, and write:

train	trailer
paint	grain
sail	rail
painter	tail

2. Give the children a paper with sketches and missing vowels. The sketches will tell them what the word is. Some **ea** words are included. Duplicating Master No. 24 is similar to this exercise.

3. For writing, have the children complete these sentences. Answers may also be on the board in random order. Include two extra words with answers for better thought processes. (*gain, sail*)

Put water in a _____. (*pail*)
Hens eat _____. (*grain*)
If milk spills, it will _____. (*stain*)
The pig has a little _____. (*tail*)
If we eat fast, we get a _____. (*pain*)

Workbook page 32 follows this lesson.

Enrichment

providing enrichment activities

Stories: Lenski, Lois, *The Little Airplane,* Oxford.
The Little Sail Boat, Oxford.
The Little Train, Oxford.

Piper, Watty, *The Little Engine that Could,* Platt and Munk.

poems for enrichment

Poems: Bennett, Rowena B., "A Modern Dragon," and "Racing the Train," in *Around a Toadstool Table,* Follett.

Field, Rachel, "Rain," in *Taxis and Toadstools,* Doubleday.

Milne, A. A., "The Engineer," in *Now We Are Six,* Dutton.

Mitchell, Lucy S., "A Locomotive," in *Here and Now Story Book,* Dutton.

Tippett, James, "Trains," in *Sung Under a Silver Umbrella,* Macmillan.

Page 59 — A poem: An ant

Introduction

This poem has a definite rhythm and style. Read it to the class first to give them this style. The discussion motivated by the poem will probably take longer than the actual reading.

developing a sense of rhythm

Procedure

making comparisons

1. After you have read it, ask what the grass seems like to an ant; the rain puddle; the rock; a fern. If they cannot answer, have them read silently to find the answers. (*forest, sea, hill, tree*)
2. Have the group read the poem in unison; then have one or two children read it alone to the others.
3. Ask what long **e** words they can find, containing **ea** or **ee.**
4. Have other comparisons made, such as what would someone's foot seem like to the ant? an acorn? a step? What would the desk seem like to a worm? the chair to a grasshopper? Lead children to use their imaginations.

Suggestions for Further Activities

creative writing of poems

Using this poem as a pattern, other original poems may be created using a variety of familiar animals, such as a toad in the garden, a snail, or a turtle.

Page 60 — The Milk Maid and Her Pail

ed

Special group of words to be presented before the lesson. These words, for the sake of the story, are presented ahead of their regular sequence.

Procedure

reviewing pronunciation of the *ed* suffix

Put the familiar words in context: **Bob called to Tim.** Have a child read it orally and call on another child to underline **called.** Have all the children say the word. Continue with: Nan **helped** Nell dust. Follow the above procedure also with: We **steamed** the clams. Call attention to the fact that they do not hear a second syllable. Now put the new words in context and follow the same procedure.

The little lad was **named** Bill.
Pam **skipped** to the barn.
Ed **tossed** the ball.
He **spilled** his milk.

After the children have read the words in context, erase all the words but the underlined ones, and have the children find them as you pronounce them. Repeat two or three times.

Introduction

developing story background

Review the characteristics of farm or country life through a discussion of the picture. Bring out that it is probably a story about "long ago." (Our milk is now pasteurized, etc.)

Guiding Reading for Comprehension

Direct the children's attention to the title. After they have read it, the children can tell who the girl is (*a milk maid*) and that the story is also about her pail.

finding words with the long **a**

Have the children find the long **a** words. They may frame them on the page, or copy them from the book on the board. The words include: **maid, pail, named, Gail, braided, hair.** Call on the children to read the words. Ask the children what the girl's name is (*Gail*) and where she was going. (*market*) Have them read the second sentence silently, and then orally for fluency.

Page 61 — The Milk Maid and Her Pail (*continued*)

Guiding Reading for Comprehension

On the next page, ask how the little girl was moving (*skipping*), and what she was thinking about. (*trade milk for hen*) Ask who is talking on the third line? (*Gail*) Explain that if Gail is talking about herself, she doesn't use her own name. Use the class as an example —i.e. "Bobby, if you want to tell me something about yourself, what do you say? Do you say Bobby has new shoes?" (*no*) "What do you call yourself?" (*I*) For review, call the children's attention to the **I** on the page. Ask, "What is she going to trade her milk for?" (*hen from which she would get eggs to sell*) Have the thought unit read aloud; stress having the quotation read as the girl would say it.

reviewing use of the pronoun *I*

Have the entire page read for better understanding of the story.

Page 62 — The Milk Maid and Her Pail (*continued*)

Guiding Reading for Comprehension

my

Continue the story by asking what Gail is going to sell her eggs for. (*silk dress*) Have the children recognize **silk.** It may be necessary to ask, after the first question, "What kind of dress?"

This is a good story to bring out children's reactions. Don't omit this in your discussions. Ask if the children know why Gail wants a new dress. (*so the lads will speak to her*) (This is a very long sentence.) Remind the children that they must read from the capital letter to the period for the whole sentence. Have the first sentence and the second sentence read orally. Bring out the feeling of pride displayed in the tossing of braids.

interpreting characters' actions

Special Word my

Ask the children if they see any new word on the next line. (*my*) When they have found **my,** ask if anyone can guess what it is by reading about the braids. Ask what she is going to do with her braids. (If no child can respond to **my,** ask whose braids they are and explain that if they are Gail's, and she is talking about her own braids, she would say **my.**) Give further examples by using the names of the children in the class; for example: say, "Joe's book." Joe would say, "My book." "Tom's pencil." Tom would say, "My pencil."

Have the entire page read orally.

introducing the pronoun *my*

Page 63 — The Milk Maid and Her Pail (*conclusion*)

Guiding Reading for Comprehension

or

Have the children read the first two sentences. Ask them to come and whisper to you what has happened. (*Pail fell off; milk was spilled.*) Ask those children who hesitate to point out the difficult words. Put such words as **spilled, tossed, off,** and **all** on the board and develop or review them with the children. Have the sentences read orally after the children have had time to study them silently.

checking comprehension

The last sentence has a moral. Have it read silently, and then as part of the entire page.

interpreting the moral of the story

Have the children reread the story, and discuss the moral of the story: Gail's pride and desire to show off to the lads and the other girls caused her to lose everything.

Special Word or

introducing the special word *or*

Call attention to the word at the bottom of the page. Ask the children what it is. (*or*) This word will present no difficulty for them since they have been reading **for** since page 36 of *Book A*. Have them use **or** in several sentences so that you are sure they know the word.

Suggestions for Further Activities

exercises for independent work

Put phrases on the board for writing or for further practice with the special words, such as:

I paid	my pail
I ate	my team
I painted	my cars
I can wait	my steed

These can be illustrated.

Workbook page 33 follows this lesson.

Duplicating Masters Nos. 25 and 26 can be used here.

Enrichment

Story: "Mr. Vinegar," in Huber, *I Know a Story,* Row, Peterson.

Page 64 — Recognition of long i and ie

phoneme-grapheme relationships

Building Linguistic Skills

Introduction of long **i,** using signal **e,** and the **ie** digraph.

Introduction

introducing the long **i** phoneme

Review the two rules concerning recognition of long **i,** i.e. *signal e* and *vowel digraph.*

Note: The teacher may use the term *vowel digraph* after explaining that it is two vowels which come together to make the sound of *one* of them. If she prefers to omit the linguistic term, she need only say that when two vowels come together we *usually* hear the long sound of the first vowel.

Procedure

1. Make a game of changing words:

changing words with short **i** to words with long **i**

Tim	___	time
kit	___	kite
rid	___	ride
pin	___	pine
spin	___	spine

Have the class read the words as you build them, either on the board or by adding **e** to flash cards.

2. Change **mill** to **mile** and **still** to **stile,** and ask what change the children have noticed. Ask for volunteers to write **till** and then change it to **tile;** similarly change **pill** to **pile,** and **fill** to **file.** Before going on to the next spelling change, be sure that all the children understand that when the terminal letter is **e** and the vowel is long, we do not double the consonant. You may put a few words in context on the board as further drill:

The mill is a mile down the street.
The pill made me feel better.
Put the dimes in a pile.
I will fill the file with letters.

Have the children read each sentence as you write it. After all the sentences are on the board, have the children underline the long **i** words.

3. Use the same steps as suggested above to bring out changes in spelling from **Dick** to **dike, lick** to **like,** and **pick** to **pike.** Have the children spell or write:

Mike
strike
bike
hike
spike

Note: It may be necessary to explain again that **k** without **c** is used with a signal **e.**

adding *er* to words with long **i**

4. Put **dine** on the board; after the children have read it, add **r,** and again have the children read it. Do this with **fine, line, ripe, wide, time, bite, smile, ride,** and **mine.** Call attention to the sound of the **er,** showing that when there is only one consonant before the **er,** the **e** is usually serving two purposes: it is also a signal **e** to tell you that the words have a long **i.**

developing vocabulary

5. Use many words in short phrases for rapid word recognition, fluency, and understanding. Here are some suggestions:

mine is red	bite the meat	hide the bike
a pine tree	all my life	ripe plums
a fine mill	a black line	a pile of grass
ride in a car	at his side	strike the ball

Note: With most average or above average groups, the rules taught here give enough power for decoding other words. However, with slower groups, it may be necessary to provide more visual exercises, either with flash cards or with words in context. Here are additional phrases.

ride a bike	a big spike
here is mine	inside the barn
a pile of sticks	cost a dime
a bite of apple	nine miles
a fine kite	the bride smiles

Workbook page 34 can be used here.

building discrimination of long **i** and short **i** words

6. It is suggested that this be the beginning of a new lesson. Explain to the children that we have some words which do not go by the rules. We cannot tell that they have long **i**, but we must try both ways to see which makes sense. Put **find** on the board. Call on a child to read it. If the response is **find** with a short **i**, ask if the child knows what it means. Has anyone heard such a word? If not, suggest the child try a long **i**. He will recognize **find** immediately. Continue with **kind, mind, bind, grind,** and—a more difficult one—**behind.** After the children have read these words, put *I will wind my top* on the board and have a child read it. Then write *The wind fills the sails.* As they read, they will find it necessary to change to the short **i** to make sense. This is the only way to identify the sound in these words—to put them in context:

The man is blind.		Wind up the little car.
the winter wind		The dog limps on his hind leg
mind me	a kind man	a kind of cake

Have the children find and mark all the long **i's.** Here are some additional words which can be used: **mint, lint, pint, blimp, link,** and **kink.**

introducing the digraph **ie**

7. If the unusual words above have been taught with the signal **e** words, it is recommended that the next group of words be taught in a new lesson. If not, they may be combined with step 6. Recall the vowel digraph rule as you put on the board the sentence, *I like pie.* Have the children find the long **i's.** When they find the long **i** in **pie,** have them draw a line around **ie** and read the sentence. Carry out similar activities to introduce the other words in the manual:

See my silk tie.
I will lie here.
Ann cried for a cake.
We dried her tears.
Tom fried the clams.
We tried to make the kite go up.

8. Return to the book, page 64, and review all the words on the page. Clarify the meanings of such words as: **stile, swine, stride**, etc.

developing word meanings

Suggestions for Further Activities

exercises for independent work

1. The following list can be copied by the children. They may mark the **i** either *long* or *short*. Marks may be diacritical, or words labeled **l** and **s**.

win– *short*	pie
skin	pin
time	liner
fine	stick

2. A similar list can be used with the vowels omitted. The child may supply the vowel. This lesson should be checked with the children to see that they have written a word and can read it.

h__re	g__me
n__me	p__pe
d__re	P__te
t__me	l__fe

3. Put the following list on the board; have the children change the vowel to a long sound, write the word, and illustrate it on their papers:

pin	mill	dim	rip
kit	pill	till	bit

Duplicating Master No. 27 follows this lesson.
Workbook pages 35 and 36 follow this lesson.

Page 65 — Words having ir and ire

Building Linguistic Skills

phoneme-grapheme relationships

Phoneme resulting from **r** following **i;** the change when signal **e** is added to **ir.**

Introduction

Show pictures mounted on oaktag (9″ x 12″) to the class—each picture labeled: *girl, bird, fir, first grade.* Have the children read the word through recognition of the picture, or say the word and have the children repeat it after you.

Procedure

1. Ask what sound they hear in every word. (*ir*) Then ask what they see in every word which is the same. (*i, r*) Tell the children that the **r** changes the sound of the **i** to the sound they hear.

introducing the **ir** pattern

2. Have the children frame with their hands the **ir** sound. Put the same words on the board; have the children draw a line around the **ir** sound and read the word.

3. Develop the remaining words in this group from the known words, i.e.:

fir __ firm
fir __ sir
fir __ dirt, etc.

introducing the **ire** pattern

4. Recall the function of signal **e;** put **fir** on the board, add **e,** and have the children apply the signal **e** rule and read the word. Do the same with **sir.**

clarifying word meanings

5. Direct the children to open their books to page 65. Have them pronounce all the words. Clarify the meanings by having the children use the words in sentences. If there are any words which are not understood, take the time to use them in sentences and explain their meanings. A simple explanation is enough. For example: **sire** is a word that was used many years ago when someone spoke to a king, or a servant spoke to his master. A **spire** is a tall part of a building, like a church steeple. **Tire** has two meanings: a tire for a car, and to feel tired.

6. Have the children close their books; supply them with paper. Dictate the words in random order. After the children have had time to write the words, choose a child to write his words on the board. Guide the children in checking their own work.

Suggestions for Further Activities

developing creative writing skills

Many easy words have been taught, and the children who do manuscript writing should be encouraged now to take simple stories of two or three sentences from dictation. They should also begin to create their own stories, using capital letters, periods, and question marks.

Easy picture books with accompanying short stories can be compiled for a class-sharing activity. Unlearned words used in the story can be spelled by the teacher. Many children will be able to read them in context. Original sentences, like: *I like to swim in the summer,* or *I like to play ball,* lend themselves to good illustrations.

composing nonsense jingles

Nonsense jingles can also be fun. They can be dictated or originated by the children. The teacher can give the first line and have the children create the rhyming one, as:

"I saw a tiny mouse,
He ran into my house."

The teacher may wish to use a variety of techniques for these jingles. They are amusing to illustrate and give good opportunities for class sharing. Some oral suggestions for first lines are:

"A wee little cat _____"
"My furry little pup _____"
"The funny fat pig _____"
"A tiny green bug _____"
"A little gray mole _____"
"A busy old rat _____"

Suggestions for Further Activities

Workbook page 37 follows this lesson.
Duplicating Master No. 28 also follows.

Page 65 — Time for Bed

Introduction

sharing personal experiences

Discuss the picture; then encourage the children to relate similar personal experiences. It is usually necessary to insist that the children speak loudly enough for all the class to hear. Children have a tendency to talk just to the teacher. This picture lends itself to a storytelling time. As the children relate personal experiences, they should use complete sentences and correct grammar, should speak in a pleasant voice, and should organize their thoughts. However, it is not a good idea to interrupt the children to correct errors. Often repeating the sentence after a child, directing it to the whole group, and merely using corrected grammar, teaches by usage without calling attention to the child's error.

Guiding Reading for Comprehension

reviewing the title

Direct attention to the title. This title does not tell who is in the story. Point out that the title is short, not a whole sentence, and tells what the story is about. After silent reading, have the title read aloud.

The first sentence tells who the boys are. Have the children find the names. (*Bill and Mike*) Give even the slowest children time to read silently this two-line sentence. Then have it read aloud.

Have the children find who is talking in the next two sentences. (*Bill*) After silent reading, ask a child to read the words that Bill said just as he thinks Bill said them. Ask, "Who says he will be in bed first?"

Page 66 — Time for Bed (*continued*)

Guiding Reading for Comprehension

checking comprehension

Have the children find the word that describes how Mike put out the lamp. (*snapped*) Ask how many parts they hear in *snapped*. (Have them clap their hands if necessary.)

Ask what kind of bed Bill and Mike had. (*fine*) Find other words that describe the bed. (*big, wide*)

locating the **ai** digraph

The last sentence is a difficult one. Have the children pick out the *ai* vowel digraph words (*raised, pair*), study, and read them. Guide them in working out these words before the entire sentence is read orally. Note that here is another word (raised) that has an *ed* ending, but we hear only the *d*. Have the entire page reread before going on to the next page.

Pages 67 and 68 — Time for Bed (*continued*)

do

Introduction

drawing conclusions from picture clues

In discussing this picture, let the children draw their own conclusions as to who the man is—whether he is the father of either of the boys, a friendly policeman checking on the boys' safety, a next door neighbor, etc. Discuss the emotional reactions of the boys—scared, frightened. Discourage the use of *sad;* some children classify anything not happy as sad.

Guiding Reading for Comprehension

locating vowel sounds in the story

Have the children study the first four sentences, putting their fingers on the words as you direct them. Instruct them to find a word with an **ar** sound. (*dark*) Find a word with a long **i.** (*hide*) Find a two-syllable word. (*under, blanket*) Find a word with a vowel digraph or long **a.** (*hair*) If they point out **afraid,** some children may read it in context; however, it may also be developed linguistically. Cover the **a**, and have the children discover the second syllable. Then allow them to see the whole word. Ask what **a** "says" as a word. (*short u*) Explain that it often has the same sound at the beginning of a word because **it is not stressed u fraid.** Have the last sentence read aloud.

Have the children read the first sentence on page 68 to find out what the boys did.

Special Word do

Continue the silent reading to learn what Mike told Bill to do. Have the word *do* identified, as this word is used out of order for the sake of the story. Have the thought unit read aloud (three sentences). Have the last thought unit read silently, and then have the entire page read aloud for fluency and continuity.

introducing the special word *do*

Pages 69 and 70 — Time for Bed (*conclusion*)

Guiding Reading for Comprehension

Ask the children to find out who speaks first on page 69. (*the man*) Ask them to find the word that tells how he talked. (*cried*) Point out that this means excitement. What did Mike and Bill do? (*ran from the tent*) Who was the man? (*Farmer Tom*) Who saw him first? (*Bill*) (Page 70) Have a child read aloud the sentence that tells what Farmer Tom had with him. (*spade*) What did he do with the spade? (*dug and tossed dirt*) Ask what Bill thought about Farmer Tom, and why. (*fine, came in time,* etc.)

checking comprehension

Reread the story for continuity. There are several quotations in this story. Encourage good expression by telling the children to say the words just as they think Farmer Tom or Bill or Mike did.

oral reading for expression

Use this opportunity to discuss safety, fire prevention, and the need for adult supervision. Several excellent safety lessons can be initiated at the conclusion of this story.

Workbook page 38 follows this lesson.

Duplicating Masters Nos. 29 and 30 also may be used.

Page 71 — The long o sound

Building Linguistic Skills

phoneme-grapheme relationships

Introduction of long **o** sounds found in (1) two letter words, (2) words with signal **e,** and (3) words with long **o** followed by two consonants. Introduction of words not having long **o,** but with similar grapheme pattern.

Introduction

introducing the long **o** phoneme

Review the signal **e** rule, again using the children's names—long and short. Tell a story about a little **mole** who ran into a **hole.** He found himself **alone,** with **no** one around; **so** he decided he'd **poke** his **nose** here and there until he'd made a new **home.** Put the dark-type words on the board as you talk.

Procedure

recognizing the long **o** words with signal **e**

1. After the words have been put on the board, ask the children to find any words they recognize. (The children may recognize several words.) Repeat the word after the child, and ask what sound the **o** makes. Review the list; this time the children should be able to read all the words.

2. Point out that **go, so,** and **no** do not have a signal **e,** but if we were to try to say these words with a short **o,** they would not "make sense."

3. List the following words on the board and have the children read them: **sole, lone, pole, home, tone.** Use more words from the text if necessary to teach the children to recognize the long **o** sound easily.

teaching irregular words: *come, some, done*

4. To develop the irregular words, *come, some,* and *done,* use the following procedure.

a) Put the following sentence on the board:

I will come home alone.

Have the children read silently; then ask if any of the words are difficult. Some children may point to **come.** If so, ask them to try the long sound; "does it make sense?" "Try the short sound—does it make sense? This is an irregular word with a special sound. What word would be missing if you read the remainder of the sentence?" (Cover **come** with your hand and call on a child to read: I will _____ home alone.) Obtain **come** as the response to the question. Put several phrases on the board:

come here
he can come

come again
come to me

b) Follow a similar procedure to teach **some**. A suggested sentence is: *Here are some stones.*
c) A similar procedure should follow to introduce **done**: *Is my cake done?* or *Has Tom done his tasks?*
d) Flash cards with these three words should be interspersed with long **o** (signal **e**) words for rapid recognition.

5. The introduction of vowels made long when followed by two consonants can be the beginning of a new lesson if in the teacher's judgment steps 1 to 4 are enough for one lesson. Explain that some long **o** words do not require a signal **e**. Use the words in context:

recognizing long **o** words without signal **e**

Dan has the most fun at ball games.

Have the children study silently, read aloud, and then mark the long **o**. Here are suggested sentences for several of the words used in the text:

The colt did not leave the mare's side.
A man is a host in his home.
Will you hold my rope?
The gun is in a holster.

Duplicating Master No. 31 can be used here. The pictures represented are:

exercises for independent work

rose	kite	cake
gate	cone	pipe
dime	home	cape

Duplicating Master No. 32 also follows this lesson.
Workbook pages 39, 40, and 41 can be used here.

Page 72 — Words having or and ore

Introduction

In introducing the **or** words with signal **e**, you should have little difficulty in getting the children to read the words directly from the text. If any of these words presents a problem, discuss and present one on the board—"My cut finger is **sore**."

introducing **or** words with signal **e**

Procedure

Explain that most words with **or** have a spelling without signal **e**, as:

introducing **or** words without signal **e**

I want cake **for** supper.
I need a **fork** to eat it.
It is Ned's **or** Tom's.

Use the board if necessary to present the words in context; otherwise, turn to page 72 to have the children read the lists of words. Have the children use the words in sentences if there is a difficult meaning. If the children do not recognize the meaning of such words as **lore** and **ford,** you should tell them.

developing word meanings

Suggestions for Further Activities

building vowel discrimination

1. To correlate reading and writing have the children copy the following list, supplying long or short marks: (You may prefer to have the children use L and S rather than the diacritical marks – and ⌣.)

sob	hole	post	home
lock	toss	hot	bond
tone	robe		

exercises for independent work

2. Have the children select, from page 72, eight (or any number designated) words which they can illustrate. Be sure they label the pictures.

3. Put simple but interesting sentences on the board to be illustrated. Examples:

The smoke rose behind the tent.
The cork will bob on the water.
The cow hand has a rope on his saddle.
The corn is ripe now.
The robe has some roses on it.
The man stole a horse.
We call a mailman a postman.

Let the children choose the ones they wish to illustrate. You may assign one, two, or even four, but they should not be expected to do more than that. Additional assignments will often result only in poor work habits.

Duplicating Master No. 33 follows this lesson.

Workbook pages 42 and 43 may be used here.

Enrichment

providing enrichment

Poem: Milne, A. A., "Jonathan Jo," in *When We Were Very Young,* Dutton.

Page 73 — A poem: A Little Elf

Introduction

Allow the children time to enjoy the illustration. Ask for the names by which this little person is known—gnome, elf, brownie, fairy, etc.

enjoying the illustration

Procedure

1. Have the children read the poem silently. Ask them to point out words that give difficulty.
2. Ask for pairs of rhyming words.
3. Ask what words have long **o** sounds. (*alone, acorn,* and *home* are included although *acorn* is properly pronounced ā′côrn.)
4. Have the group read the poem in unison.
5. Have several children read it alone for pleasure. Stress fluency and rhythm.

reading with rhythm

Duplicating Masters Nos. 34 and 35 follow this lesson.

Enrichment

There are many poems that are simple but charming about elves and fairies in the Arbuthnot Anthology, *Time for Poetry,* published by Scott, Foresman.

providing enrichment activities

Page 74 — The Lost Cow

Introduction

A discussion of the pictures will bring out that the story is about a cowboy, his horse, his holster, and his gun. "Where do you think the cowboy is going? Why does he need a rope?" (*to rope calves or strays*) "—a gun and holster?" (*to shoot those animals, snakes, or wildcats which might attack his cattle*) "—a cowboy hat?" (*to protect him from the sun, wind, and rain; to hold food; to dip water from a creek; to use in many ways*).

developing story background

Guiding Reading for Comprehension

As the children study the title ask what the story is about. Ask. "Does this tell us a little about where the cowboy may be going What word tells what has happened to the cow?" (*lost*) Discuss again the characteristics of a good title.

discussing a good title

Direct the children to find out what the cowboy's name is, (*Ted Lane*) and where he is going. (*into the hills*) Have them read the first two sentences silently and aloud.

finding vowel sounds in the story

The fourth paragraph is long and difficult. It will require analysis—what are the long **a** words? (*braided, nail*) What is the long **e** word? (*near*) What two-syllable words do you see? (*braided, corral, saddle*) If the children have difficulty with "corral," ask the name of the fenced-in yard where the cowboys keep their horses. Have the class find and point to **corral.** Following the study, have the sentence read orally. With the last sentence, give an opportunity for silent reading; then ask, "For what is the cowboy going to use his rope?" (*to rope the lost cow*)

Have the entire page read aloud. Work for fluency in reading the two-line sentences.

Page 75 — The Lost Cow (*continued*)

Introduction

Discuss the picture and the tracks around the water hole. What kind of tracks might they be?

Guiding Reading for Comprehension

checking comprehension

Direct the children to read the first complete thought unit silently (two sentences). Ask whose tracks Ted saw. (*his cow's*) Direct the class to the next thought unit (two sentences). After silent reading, ask, "Why is Ted eager to find his cow soon?" (*wants to find her before dark*)

Ask the children to find an **or** word in the next sentence. (*more*) After silent reading, ask, "What is around the water hole?" (*sand and wet grass*) Have the children complete the page silently. Ask. "Does Ted think he can find his cow?" (*yes*) "Why?" (*because of the tracks*) Have the entire page read orally. Turn immediately to page 76 to keep the story moving.

Page 76 — The Lost Cow (*continued*)

making deductions from picture clues

Introduction

In discussing the picture, ask if the children think this man has found Ted's cow and is taking care of her for Ted. The man's character is shown by his dress, etc. In discussing this man's appearance, and what he seems to be, you are developing the comprehension skill of forming opinions or making deductions from picture clues.

Guiding Reading for Comprehension

This is a rather short page, with very few difficulties. Ask the children to read the whole page silently to find out why the man has the cow, but if the children can do it, by all means have them read it aloud without study. After all have finished (ask the children to look up when they have finished the page), get the answer to the first question; (*stole the cow*) then ask how they think Ted will get the cow.

reading an entire page silently

Have the page read aloud.

Page 77 — The Lost Cow (*conclusion*)

Introduction

Here, the picture reveals the outcome of the story. Turn the children's attention immediately to the story and discuss the picture after the reading.

Guiding Reading for Comprehension

Ask which word tells how Ted spoke to the man. (*cried*) See if the children can recall where this word was used previously. (*Time for Bed,* page 69) Then ask, "What other word tells almost the same thing?" (*called*) In this type of guided reading, the child reads to the point where he finds the answer. After the question has been answered, the teacher gives another question, and the children continue their silent reading. Here are suggested questions:

reading to answer specific questions

What did Ted do with his rope? (*spun*)
How did it go through the air? (*sailed*)
What two words (in the fourth sentence) have long **o's**? (*hope, rope*)
Where will Ted go next? (*home*)
What word describes the man? (*bad*)
Did Ted get his cow? What did he use? (*rope*)

Discuss the duties of cowboys, such as branding, repairing fences, feeding the cattle in the winter, and many other duties which do not relate to "bad men," rustling, etc. Numerous stories, including the "Cowboy Sam" series, bring out the interesting and varied life of the cowboy.

developing story background

Suggestions for Further Activities

exercises for independent work

1. Many illustrations may be created directly from the cowboy discussion. If this story is used to motivate a regular art lesson, a colorful bulletin board or display can be made with crayoned pictures on 12″ x 18″ paper, cut colored construction paper on 12″ x 18″ paper, or tempera paint on 18″ x 24″ paper.

finding rhyming words

2. Use rhyming exercises and correlate them with writing. Put a list of words on the board, and then put a rhyming list in random order beside it. Have the children copy the lists and draw a line from each word in the first column to the one that rhymes in the second:

nose	sail
smoke	wide
hail	rose
ride	seed
feed	poke

3. If a mimeographed sheet can be given out, it is suggested that the page be divided and not more than five word pairs be put in each box, for example:

cake	bee	cold	team	find	liner
see	make	dream	train	diner	pail
die	hole	rain	tire	fail	seat
mole	pie	fire	bold	beat	kind

supplying rhyming words

4. The following list of words may be given to the children either on the board or on a mimeographed sheet. Direct the children to supply a rhyming word for each. In some cases, it will be necessary to allow the children to use their books for reference:

alone	______
sail	______
tree	______
horn	______
cork	______
most	______
mind	______
rake	______

Workbook page 44 is a comprehension check of the story. Workbook page 45 is similar to exercises 3 and 4 above.

Enrichment

Stories: Lenski, Lois, *Cowboy Small,* Oxford.
Chandler, Edna W., "Billy and the Cowboys," in the *Cowboy Sam* series, Beckley-Cardy.

Poems: Roberts, Elizabeth Madox, "Milking Time," in *Sung Under the Silver Umbrella,* Macmillan.
Stevenson, R. L., "The Cow," in *A Child's Garden of Verses,* Oxford.

providing enrichment activities

Page 78 — Vowel digraphs oa and oe

does

Introduction

Review the pattern of two vowels coming together and tell the children that this new group of vowels (or digraphs) will make it possible for them to read many new words.

phoneme-grapheme relationships

At all times, remember that almost without exception first-grade children have a strong desire to learn to read. This desire, plus pride in their own reading ability, provides intrinsic motivation which is better than most artificial devices. Your enthusiasm as the children show success will carry the pace of your lesson. You must show outward enthusiasm for little children. This is contagious. If you react to their growth in reading, they will appreciate the importance of what they are accomplishing.

developing enthusiasm for reading

Procedure

1. Put **oa** on the board, or, if you wish, turn directly to the text. Have the children "guess" the sound. As soon as it has been established as long **o**, go immediately into word recognition. This should not be difficult since the words present little difficulty either in spelling or in meaning.

introducing the **oa** and **oe** digraphs

2. Explain that **oe** has the same sound as **oa** and have the children read the words in the book.

3. **Does** is a special word. Have the children look at it and say what they think it is. Ask if they know any word like that. Have they ever heard such a word? Put the following sentence on the board: *Ned does not like milk.* Have the children read it silently; then ask if anyone thinks he can read the sentence. After a child has read it aloud, point to **does** and call on a child to say the word. Be sure all the children see and hear the word. Put *Does Ann like milk?* on the board and have the children read it silently. Then have a child read it aloud. Call on a child to frame **does.** Explain

teaching the special word *does*

playing a rapid recognition game

that this is spelled like the **oe** words but has an exceptional pronunciation.

4. Play a short game for rapid recognition, either with flash cards or in any drill form that you have found profitable, so that the children do not spend time painfully sounding out words. Establishing the phoneme-grapheme pattern thoroughly should result in rapid recognition. Always allow the child to think through the word silently; then, when he pronounces it, he should be able to say it as a whole. Do not encourage "sounding out" aloud, and never have them pronounce the initial sound without the following vowel sound.

Suggestions for Further Activities

exercises for independent work

1. Many of these words are easily illustrated. Put on the board sentences that require more detail in the pictures than has been suggested previously, for example:

A toad is in the road.
The oars are in the boat.
The goat eats grain.
Put some soap in the water.

building creative writing skills: nonsense jingles

2. Have the children write jingles which can also be illustrated and made up into a book. The teacher may begin by giving a first line or asking the children to give a sentence ending with one of the words from the page. Example: *He put on his coat.* Then have the children create the second line. It can be nonsense. This is fun for everyone.

"He put on his coat
And jumped in the boat."

The children can copy several jingles from the board for practice in writing and then make their own books. Some are included on page 48 of the workbook.

3. Give the children mimeographed sheets with the first lines and part of the second lines. They must supply the last word as suggested in the previous game. Include the words from this page.

Duplicating Master No. 36 follows this lesson.

Workbook pages 46 and 47 also follow this lesson.

Enrichment

providing enrichment activities

Stories: Burgess, Thornton W., *The Adventures of Old Mr. Toad,* Little.

Poems: Bennett, R. B., "Boats," in *Around a Toadstool Table,* Follett.

Rossetti, Christina, "The Bridge," in *Sing Song,* Macmillan.

Pages 79 and 80 — The Sad Goat

Introduction

once

A brief discussion of the picture may serve to introduce the story. However, the title will elicit more curiosity about what is going to happen than the illustration. Have the children discover the title and read to find out why the goat is sad.

using the title to motivate reading

Guiding Reading for Comprehension

Note that this story introduces the full paragraph with sentences starting anywhere on a line. In guiding the children, have them recognize the capital letter as the beginning and the period as the end of the sentence. As you explain about the capital letter and the period (or question mark, etc.), use the word "sentence" and tell the children that a sentence tells a complete thought. It is about something, and tells what that something did. Give a few examples of phrases and sentences aloud, such as, "the little red wagon." Ask, "What is this about?" (*little red wagon* or *wagon*) "What did it do?" (*It doesn't tell.*) Say, "The little red wagon rolled down the hill," and discuss the subject and the action. Several phrases may be put on the board either before or after the oral reading to give further experiences with a complete sentence. The children read and notice that the phrases are not complete. You may have to ask, "What did it do? What happened to it?" to complete them. Here are some suggestions:

introducing the full paragraph

understanding sentence structure

My red car _______
Mother's green dress _______
Ned's little boat _______

Work for fluency in phrasing and correct intonation at the end of the sentences.

Call the children's attention to the first phrase (four words) and have someone read these words aloud. Since the special word **once** may be unfamiliar to children in the group, the teacher may have to read the phrase, "once upon a time." Put **once** on the board, and add a flash card to those which the children are using for further review.

introducing the special word *once*

Ask what kind of story this is going to be. (*fairy story, make-believe,* etc.) Have them find the **oa** words in the first paragraph. As a child finds a word, he may write it on the board. Have the children read these words. Ask, "What words describe the goat?" (*old, fat, black as coal*) Continue the study of the second paragraph by asking, "What does the goat want to do?" (*hop like a toad*)

checking comprehension

On page 80, ask who is talking in the first paragraph. (*oak tree*) Ask, "Does he think the goat will be able to hop? (*no*) Does he think anything can hop? (*yes, a frog*) How can you tell now that this is really a make-believe story?" (*the animals and the tree talk*) The time taken in discussion of true and untrue stories is rich and well spent. This story is the first of this kind.

oral reading with expression

Have the pages read aloud; stress expression. Have one child "be" the goat, one the tree, and one the narrator. Perhaps "playing" the story will lead to other animal plays.

Page 81 — The Sad Goat (*continued*)

Introduction

enjoying the humor

Let the children enjoy the humor of the picture before getting to the words. They will be eager to continue the story.

Guiding Reading for Comprehension

Ask the children to find a word in the first paragraph which means the same as **hop.** (*leap*) Continue silent reading with as few questions as possible.

Have the children read page 81 silently to learn what happened to the goat.

dramatic reading of the story

Have the pages read aloud for fun. Perhaps children will want to "play" out the whole story. Let many children take the parts to sustain interest.

Discuss the moral of the story—boasting. Did the goat learn a lesson? This story could lead into the reading of some of the simple fables, like "The Fox and the Grapes."

Suggestions for Further Activities

creative writing activity

1. The logical activity here would be a study of the fables, or an opportunity for creative stories involving things that talk. Encourage the children to tell stories (three sentences) having an animal or an inanimate object talk—*a house, a boat, a tree,* etc. Some of these stories may be recorded by the teacher for a class book, a writing lesson, or a drawing lesson.

developing discrimination of nouns and verbs

2. A worksheet activity can be included here to help the children become aware of things they can see or touch, and things they can do. This is the beginning of a recognition of nouns and verbs using the meaning of a noun or verb rather than its grammatical term. Give the children a worksheet similar to the following one. Have the children cut off the words and paste them under the correct heading according to whether they are names of things or action words.

See	Do
run	swim
skip	make
boat	spin
doll	grass
cake	goat

Duplicating Master No. 37 follows this lesson.
Workbook pages 49 and 50 also follow.

Enrichment

Include, as well as the fables mentioned below, some of the simple stories with talking characters.

providing fables for enrichment

Stories and Tales: *Aesop's Fables,* from the Translation of Thomas James and George Tyler Townsend, Lippincott.

Crampton, Gertrude, *Scuffy, the Tug Boat,* Golden Press.

Piper, Watty, *The Little Engine That Could,* Platt and Munk.

Wiggin, Mrs. Kate Douglas, and Smith, Nora Archibald, *Talking Beasts, A Book of Fable Wisdom,* Doubleday.

Page 82 — Recognition of the j sound

phoneme-grapheme relationships

Building Linguistic Skills

Recognition of **j** and addition of words having this letter to vocabulary.

enjoying simple poems

Introduction

Have the children say some of the familiar Mother Goose rhymes with you. Include "Jack be Nimble" and "Jack and Jill." Read or teach "Jonathan Jo" from A. A. Milne's *When We Were Very Young*. After the children have recited and enjoyed the poems, list the names of the people on the board: *Jack, Jill,* and *Jonathan Jo*.

Procedure

building auditory discrimination of the **j** phoneme

1. Have the children say each name after you. Continue with the following list:

jump	just	jam
jet	Jenny	jar
jelly	Jean	jug

2. Ask the children for words beginning with this sound. List them on the board. If the children give words beginning with soft **g**, like **ginger**, explain that these words start with **g** although they have the same sound. List them separately on the board.

developing vocabulary

3. Ask the following questions; all answers must begin like **Jack**:

The name of a very fast airplane. (*jet*)
Something which holds pickles, or jelly, or peanut butter. (*jar*)
A story which makes us laugh. (*joke*)
The name of a month. (*June, January, July*)
Another word for leap. (*jump*)

4. Give a brief discriminatory drill in listening for the **j** sound. Give instructions as to how the class is to respond.

car	move	Bob	Jill	lamb	saw
run	jump	Joe	Peg	jam	say
jeep	run	Tom	Nan	ham	jaw

writing words with the **j** phoneme

5. Dictate words either for board work or for written work at the seats. Here is a suggested list:

jet	jug	Jim
job	jerk	Jack
just	jab	Jan
jump	joke	Jill

Choose words from the text. Check the work with the children immediately. This can be done by having a child put the correct spelling on the board after all have finished.

developing vocabulary meanings

6. Present the words on page 82, with discussion, illustration, and sample sentences. Many words may have to be used by you in sentences. For example:

To be fair means to be *just*.
Just also means exact, or exactly.
"This tastes *just* right."
"The judge gave him a *just* punishment."

Don't *jog* my elbow when I am writing.
We *jogged* along in the pony cart.

The logs were so closely packed, they couldn't be moved in the river. We call this a *jam*.
Sometimes the paper gets *jammed* in the machine (typewriter, etc.).
Strawberry *jam* is sweet and sticky and good on toast.

The rubbish we throw out is *junk*. A type of Chinese sailboat is a *junk*.

Suggestions for Further Activities

exercises for independent work

1. Mimeograph simple riddles; the child either draws the answer or chooses the correct answer from a group of words. For example:

I went up a hill. I got some water in my pail. I fell down. I am Jan Jack Jed Jim	I am a car. I am little. I can go in sand and in forests. I can go up hills and down. I am a jet jug jeep jest
I hold water. I can hold cold milk. I am a kind of bottle. I am a jot jug just rug	I am a name. I am a girl's name. I am like bean. Jean seen Jill Joan

playing the "Jack" game

providing enrichment activities

These riddles are similar to the workbook, page 53.

2. Put words on the board, omitting vowels. Allow the children to use their books and complete a real word:

j__b	j__g	j__st
j__nk	j__rk	j__ke

3. Play the "Jack" game. Answers to all the questions must begin with *Jack*.

Who fell down the hill? (*Jack and Jill*)
Who sat in a corner and ate pie? (*Jack Horner*)
What gives us light at Halloween? (*Jack-o'-lantern*)
Who jumped out of a box? (*Jack-in-the-box*)
Who paints your windows at night? (*Jack Frost*)

Duplicating Master No. 38 follows this lesson.
Workbook pages 51, 52, and 53 follow this lesson.

Enrichment

Poems: A. A. Milne, "Jonathan Jo," in *When We Were Very Young,* Dutton.
Laura Richards, "The Baby Goes to Boston," in Arbuthnot, *Time for Poetry,* Scott, Foresman.

Page 83 — Ride in a Jet Plane

using personal experiences as story background

Introduction

A discussion of the picture will include reading the name of the plane and discussing it. Time should be provided here for personal experience stories.

checking comprehension

Guiding Reading for Comprehension

Have the title read; then have the children find the name of the boy. (*Jack*) Ask these questions after the children have read the paragraph silently: "Where was he going? Had he ever been in a plane before?" (*West Falls, no*)

Guide the children to read the description of a jet plane in the second paragraph and finish the page silently. Have the children find the descriptive words in the paragraph. (*big, sleek*) Have the page read aloud.

Page 84 — Ride in a Jet Plane (*continued*)

Guiding Reading for Comprehension

guiding silent reading

Guide the children in silent reading. Have them point to any words they do not know. List these words on the board and have the children help each other. Some may have difficulty with **pilot** and **hostess.** Analyze these words. If no child has difficulty, put each word on the board and ask a child to read it. Be sure that all the children are ready for silent reading.

Check comprehension with questions such as: "What safety device does Jack have?" (*seat belt*) "What is the pilot's job?" (*run the Star Fire*) "What is the hostess' job?" (*help Jack*)

avoiding elaborate sounding

Have the page read aloud. Watch for any labored "sounding." If this is apparent, use flash cards during a drill period for more rapid recognition.

Pages 85 and 86 — Ride in a Jet Plane (*conclusion*)

Guiding Reading for Comprehension

developing speed in silent reading

Have the children read to answer a question for each paragraph. Work for *rapid* silent reading.

Suggested questions: "How does Jack call the hostess?" (*press a button*) "What did Jack eat?" (*meat, rolls, jam*) "What else can he do on the plane?" (*read, sleep*) "Was the Star Fire early, late, or on time?" (*on time*) "Who met Jack at the airport?" (*Jan*) "How did he get to Jan's home?" (*jeep*) "Did Jack like his ride on the jet?" (*yes*) Have the page read aloud; then have the entire story reread.

A discussion of airplane travel is the logical conclusion of the story.

Suggestions for Further Activities

exercises for independent work

1. Inaugurate flash card games between small groups with a pupil leader, or allow the children to use flash cards in pairs, checking each other. Be sure that **j** words are included with the cards.

2. Further practice in sentence recognition can be included here. Give the children a worksheet of phrases and sentences. They will read each one and determine whether it is a sentence or phrase. They may put a period at the end of each sentence and leave a

practicing sentence recognition

phrase with no mark at the end. Here are some suggestions for phrases and sentences:

Jack rode in his big red car
The sleek jet plane
Jean can jump and run
Jack and Jill
Ned will kick the ball
He can run fast
Once I
A jar of jam
We lost the oar
The fat old toad

Duplicating Master No. 39 duplicates this exercise.

Workbook page 54 may be used following this lesson and is a comprehension check of the story. Workbook page 55 gives further practice with sentence structure.

Enrichment

providing enrichment activities

Stories: Gramatky, Hardy, *Loopy,* Putnam's.
Lenski, Lois, *The Little Airplane,* Oxford.
Phleger, Frederick, *Ann Can Fly,* Random.
Whitehouse, *Real Book of Airplanes,* Doubleday.

Poems: Green, Mary M., "Aeroplane," in Arbuthnot, *Time for Poetry,* Scott, Foresman.
Tippett, James, "Up in the Air," in Arbuthnot, *Time for Poetry,* Scott, Foresman.

Page 87 — Recognition of the v sound

Building Linguistic Skills

phoneme-grapheme relationships

Recognition of the sound of *v* as an initial sound, terminal sound, and within a word. The addition of these words to the reading vocabulary.

Introduction

introducing the **v** phoneme

Cut out a large red heart and write a small and large **v** on it. Hold it up and say, "This is a *valentine*." Have the children repeat *valentine*. Be sure that the children are putting an **n** sound at the end of the word, and not an **m** sound.

Procedure

1. Follow this activity with the list below, having the children place the teeth firmly on the lower lip and exaggerate the sound:

voice	victrola	vacant
violet	victory	very
violin	vaccination	vinegar

2. Have the children identify words beginning with **v** in the following list. The response can be any action the teacher chooses. (Note that these words have been selected for fine auditory discrimination. Enunciate them very clearly):

building auditory discrimination of initial **v** phoneme

went	fairy	vouch	foal	vigor
vent	leery	pouch	volt	wiggle
find	very	found	fork	finger

3. Have the children hear **v** as a terminal sound. Have them say **stove, love, give, have, dive, cove, rave,** and **move.**

medial and terminal **v** phonemes

4. Have the children repeat the following words: **Rover, Dover, cover, over, waving,** and **diving.** Ask where they hear the **v.** (*middle*)

5. Say, *"A vest has no sleeves."* Ask which word started with **v.** Put it on the board. Continue, saying the sentences aloud as you put on the board the words that start with **v.**

We vote for our president.
A van is a big truck.
A vow is a promise.

Have the children draw a line around all the **v's** in the words listed on the board.

6. Say, *"My dog's name is Rover."* Put *Rover* on the board and have the children draw a line around the **v.** Continue with other sentences, always listing the word with **v** on the board and having the children mark that letter:

building visual discrimination of the **v** grapheme

a) He is a good *diver.*
b) Are you *saving* your money?
c) We swam in the *river.*
d) My ring is made of *silver.*
e) Does this pan *have* a *cover?*
f) The light is *over* the *stove.*
g) The *driver* wore *gloves.*
h) We will *move* to a new house.

7. Call attention to the irregular word **have** and ask if the children notice anything strange about this word. If no child notices the short **a** sound with the signal **e,** recall the signal **e** rule; then ask what vowel sound they hear in **have.**

teaching the irregular word *have*

8. On a separate part of the board, list these irregular words to be reviewed. Deal with them one at a time. **Live, give, river,** and

reviewing irregular words

liver can be treated like **have.** You can recall the others by reviewing the first list to see whether the children can detect the irregular pronunciations. If they do not hear the unusual **o** in **move** and **gloves,** it will be necessary to point it out. The irregular words **love, glove** and **dove** can be developed separately until the children are familiar with them. Flash cards should be used to develop and review this vocabulary.

developing word meanings

9. Some words, such as **vacant, eave, pave,** and **vent,** may be unfamiliar to the children, or may present some difficulty. It will be necessary to put these words on the board and develop their meaning with the children.

10. The final step in all these lessons should be a dictation of the words for written work either at the board or at the children's desks. Check the words after this lesson, so that the children can see their errors, as well as seeing the correct form.

Suggestions for Further Activities

exercises for independent work

1. List words on the board, including some special words, and have the children draw a line around the long and underline the short vowels:

vote	dive	vent	hive	five
liver	cave	have	stove	over

If you have been using the diacritical marks – and ⌣, they can be used here.

2. Give the children a duplicated sheet similar to the following, or use Duplicating Master No. 40.

using new words in sentences

Five girls _____ in my home.	(live)
	alive
	cave
We _____ a little sister.	have
	wave
See her _____ her hand.	wove
	leave
Will he _____ his ball and bat?	weave
	roves
The pup _____ milk.	loves

3. Give the children a list of words with the vowel missing; have them write a complete word:

st__ve	v__n	l__ve
w__ve	v__st	d__ve
sl__ver	v__te	g__ve
p__ve	v__lt	m__ve

supplying the missing vowel

Workbook pages 56, 57, and 58 follow this lesson.

Pages 88 and 89 — Van's Cave

Introduction

A full discussion of the illustration should precede the reading of this story. This man may be considered a hermit or a recluse—not a "bad man."

Guiding Reading for Comprehension

checking comprehension

After the title has been read, have the children study the page and be ready to answer questions. Ask, "What furniture has Van?" (*bed, stove*) "What are the bed and stove made of?" (*old lumber and old bricks*) "What is the dog's name?" (*Spot*) "Does he like this home?" (*yes*) "Why?" (*It is home.*) Have the page read aloud. It should be read by more than one child unless the class reads very easily by now.

Ask who knows the first word on page 89. (*once*) Recall the word **once.** Guide the reading of the second sentence by asking what one calls a group of ducks. After getting the answer, ask what word tells that Van shot his gun. (*fired*) Ask how many parts they hear in *fired* (*1*).

answering specific questions

Have the children read to find out what Van told Spot to do. (*Jump into the water*) Direct them to finish the page silently. Ask what word tells how Spot got into the water (*jumped*) and what they will do with the ducks. (*eat*) Continue with oral reading. Suggest that they continue the story to see whether Van and Spot enjoyed their duck dinner.

Page 90 — Van's Cave (*conclusion*)

wolf

Guiding Reading for Comprehension

Have the children study the page for one-word answers. "How was Van planning to cook the ducks?" (*roast*) "When Van went to get his ducks, where was Spot?" (*asleep*) "What did Van call Spot?" (*bad dog*) Have children read the pages aloud.

Special Word wolf

introducing the special word *wolf*

Have the children look at the illustration on page 90 and identify the animal leaving the cave. Have them find the special word **wolf** on the page. This word does not have a short **o** sound.

After this word has been identified, have the page read aloud. The entire story may be read aloud without interruption if the children seem enthusiastic about the story.

drawing conclusions

Direct the children to further study of the picture; note the feathers still remaining. "Do you think the wolf ate all the ducks? What else might he have done with them?"

Workbook pages 59, 60, 61, and the tests on pages 62 and 63 follow this lesson.

Enrichment

providing enrichment activities

Stories: All stories about "things that go" are excellent.

Burton, Virginia, *Choo Choo, Katy and the Big Snow, Mike Mulligan and His Steam Shovel,* Houghton.

Freeman, Lydia, *Chuggy and the Blue Caboose,* Viking.

Poems: Field, Rachel, "Taxis," in *Taxis and Toadstools,* Doubleday.

Duplicate this test for special words. The following words are dictated by the teacher: *her, said, been, I, my, does, once, wolf.* Have the children draw a line around each correct word. Put them in sentences if necessary.

hut her ten	see said sled	been over for	A I O
my pie sky	do toe does	on oven once	for fork wolf

Test for Spelling Dictation

The teacher dictates, but must say, "This is a vowel digraph word," or "This is the easiest spelling of a long vowel" (*signal* e), after the children have decided whether the vowel is long or short:

1. winter	___	It snows in the winter.	___	winter
2. barn	___	Cows are kept in a barn.	___	barn
3. down	___	The sled went down the hill.	___	down
4. flag	___	The flag waves overhead.	___	flag
5. plant	___	We will plant a tree.	___	plant
6. sock	___	You have a hole in your sock.	___	sock
7. milk	___	Milk is good for children.	___	milk
8. lake	___	We skate on the lake.	___	lake
9. blame	___	Who is to blame?	___	blame
10. train	___	The train is on the track.	___	train

Games for Review

Any games or devices used here for review will serve doubly if the teacher strives for fluency in phrase reading and speed in word recognition. It is fun to put phrases or sentences on the board; give the children an opportunity to read them silently and aloud, and then have them shut their eyes. Erase one word, say "Open" and see who can tell which word is gone. That child may erase the next word, and so the game continues until nearly all the words have been erased.

Put some of the more difficult words in a box (*mailbox*). A child may choose a "letter." If he can read the word he has chosen, he may keep the word until all the words have been chosen. Have the children count to see who received the largest number of letters. This game may also be played by choosing a mailman and giving him a sack. As he walks around, the child either reaches in and draws a word or he is given one by the mailman. Play as the above game.

Line some chairs up one behind the other. As the children give the correct response to the exposed flash card, they can ride on the "train."

Play "Jump the Brook," placing four or five flash cards on the floor 2′ or 3′ apart. A child reads a card, jumps over it to the next; reads it, and so on until he has safely jumped each brook. If he fails a word, he gets his feet wet—the teacher says the word and the child repeats it. He continues, then, to the other words. It is most important to remember that failure on a word should not deny him the opportunity to read the other words.

Build up Wordo Games that the children can play in small groups. As each card must be differently arranged from the others in the set, none can be duplicated. Therefore, the time involved in constructing makes it advisable to build them gradually and on firm cardboard for permanency. Here is a suggested set for special words. (Any phoneme can be reviewed. For example, long **o** and long **a** words, **k**, **c**, and **ck** words, and **ar** words.)

her	said	I	my
been	does	wolf	once
glove	home	the	a
girl	toes	plane	front

front	toes	I	said
my	plane	her	been
does	girl	wolf	a
glove	the	once	home

Make six cards similar to the two examples above. Each of these cards should be different, and should measure about 4½″ x 6″. Also a pack of 2″ x 3″ cards, each having a word, is needed. In addition the children will need markers, preferably made of small colored rectangles of paper.

The leader holds a small pack of 2″ x 3″ cards with one of these words on each card. As he calls out the word, each child covers his word with a colored marker. The first one to get a row (four words) across or down, shouts "Wordo." The leader, or teacher, should check by having the winner uncover his words one at a time, and then say them, giving the leader time to check to see that he has called all four of these words. The other children should keep their words covered so that if the first "Wordo" was in error, the game will continue. The winner becomes the next leader.

Evaluation or Check Sheet for Initial, Medial Vowel, and Terminal Sounds

This evaluation is a good inventory for future planning. Give each child a copy of the chart below. Say each of the words listed for the teacher once; the child draws a line around the correct letter for the initial sound. Repeat the word; the child draws a line around the correct letter for the vowel sound. Repeat it once more; the child draws a line around the letter for the terminal sound. *Note that these are all one-syllable words.*

For each child:

Initial			*Medial*			*Terminal*		
b	j	v	a	e	u	t	p	l
st	sl	sp	a	e	i	b	p	d
n	m	v	o	a	u	l	k	d
dr	tr	pr	a	i	e	d	b	p
c	j	g	o	a	u	j	t	l
h	l	f	o	u	a	d	b	t
bl	pl	gl	a	o	u	k	g	h
f	t	p	u	o	a	m	n	h
w	v	r	a	e	i	h	n	m
c	s	g	e	i	a	k	d	j

Words for the teacher: just, step, make, trip, goat, land, black, torn, vain, silk.

Bibliography

ENRICHMENT MATERIAL FOR BOOK B

Collections of Stories and Poems

Aesop's Fables, from the translation of James and Townsend, Philadelphia: J. B. Lippincott Co.

Arbuthnot, May Hill, *Time for Poetry,* Chicago: Scott, Foresman and Co.

Association for Childhood Education, *Sung Under the Silver Umbrella, Told Under the Magic Umbrella,* New York: The Macmillan Co.

Bailey, Carolyn Sherwin, *Merry Tales for Children,* New York: The Platt and Munk Co., Inc.

Bennett, Rowena B., *Around a Toadstool Table,* Chicago: Follett Publishing Co.

Brown, Margaret Wise, *Country Noisy Book,* Chicago: Scott, Foresman and Co.

Burgess, Thornton W., *The Adventures of Old Mr. Toad,* Boston: Little, Brown and Co.

De Huff, Elizabeth W., *Taytay's Tales,* New York: Harcourt, Brace and Co.

Field, Rachel, *Taxis and Toadstools,* Garden City, New York: Doubleday and Co., Inc.

Hubbard, Alice and Babbitt, Adeline, *The Golden Flute,* New York: The John Day Co.

Hutchinson, Veronica, *Chimney Corner Stories,* New York: G. P. Putnam's Sons.

Milne, A. A., *Now We Are Six* and *When We Were Very Young,* New York: E. P. Dutton and Co., Inc.

Mitchell, Lucy Sprague, *Here and Now Story Book* and *Another Here and Now Story Book,* New York: E. P. Dutton and Co., Inc.

Rosetti, Christina, *Sing Song,* New York: The Macmillan Co.

Stevenson, R. L., *A Child's Garden of Verses,* New York: Oxford University Press, Inc.

Wiggin, Kate Douglas and Smith, Nora Archibald, *Talking Beasts, A Book of Fable Wisdom,* Garden City, New York: Doubleday and Co., Inc.

Stories

Anderson, C. W., *Billy and Blaze,* New York: The Macmillan Co.

Beaty, John Y., *Story Pictures of Farm Animals,* Chicago: Beckley-Cardy Co.

Beim, Jerrold and Lorraine, *Two Is a Team,* New York: Harcourt, Brace and Co.

Brown, Margaret Wise, *Baby Animals,* New York: Random House, Inc.

Burton, Virginia, *Choo Choo,* Boston: Houghton Mifflin Co.
_____, *Mike Mulligan and His Steam Shovel,* Boston: Houghton Mifflin Co.
_____, *Katy and the Big Snow,* Boston: Houghton Mifflin Co.
Chandler, Edna W., *Cowboy Andy,* and *Cowboy Sam* series, Chicago: Beckley-Cardy Co.
Flack, Marjorie, *Angus and the Cat,* Garden City, New York: Doubleday and Co., Inc.
Freeman, Lydia, *Chuggy and the Blue Caboose,* New York: The Viking Press, Inc.
Gag, Wanda, *Millions of Cats,* New York: Coward-McCann, Inc.
Gramatky, Hardy, *Loopy,* New York: G. P. Putnam's Sons.
Hader, Berta and Elmer, *Cock a Doodle Doo,* New York: The Macmillan Co.
Huber, Miriam, *I Know a Story,* New York: Row, Peterson and Co.
Jackson, Kathryn and Byron, *Big Farmer Big and Little Farmer Little,* New York: Simon and Schuster, Inc.
Lenski, Lois, *Cowboy Small, The Little Airplane, The Little Farm, The Little Sailboat, The Little Train,* New York: Oxford University Press, Inc.
McCloskey, Robert, *One Morning in Maine,* New York: The Viking Press, Inc.
Meeks, Esther K., *Friendly Farm Animals,* Chicago: Follett Publishing Co.
Phleger, Frederick, *Ann Can Fly,* New York: Random House, Inc.
Piper, Watty, *The Little Engine That Could,* New York: The Platt and Munk Co., Inc.
Whitehouse, Arch, *Real Books About Airplanes,* Garden City, New York: Doubleday and Co., Inc.

Other Books

Brown, Margaret Wise, *Golden Egg Book,* New York: Simon and Schuster, Inc.
_____, *Runaway Bunny,* New York: Harper and Brothers.
Crampton, Gertrude, *Scuffy the Tug Boat,* New York: Golden Press.
Dubois, William P., *Lion,* New York: The Viking Press, Inc.
Eastman, P., *Sam and the Firefly,* New York: Random House, Inc.
Freeman, Don, *Fly High, Fly Low,* New York: The Viking Press, Inc.
Geisel, Theodor (Dr. Seuss), *And To Think That I Saw It On Mulberry St.,* New York: Vanguard Press, Inc.
Guilfoile, Elizabeth, *Nobody Listens to Andrew,* Chicago: Follett Publishing Co.
Hader, Berta and Elmer, *Farmer in the Dell,* New York: The Macmillan Co.
Hoff, Syd, *Sammy, the Seal,* New York: Harper and Brothers.
Minarik, Else H., *Father Bear Comes Home, Little Bear,* New York: Harper and Brothers.
Rey, H. A., *Curious George,* Boston: Houghton Mifflin Co.
Udry, Janice M., *A Tree Is Nice,* New York: Harper and Brothers.

Record Correlation for Basic Reading

Record Code:

A E D—Phoebe James Creative Rhythms (78 RPM)
B—Bowmar (78)
C R G—Children's Record Guild (78)
G L P—Golden Record Library (33⅓)
L E—R.C.A. Adventures in Music Series (33⅓)
M S B—Musical Sound Book Records (78)
R C A E—Albums—R.C.A. Victor Basic Educational Albums (78 or 45)
Y P R—Young People's Record Guild (78)

(Most of these records are available through

Lyons Band Instrument Co.
223 West Lake Street
Chicago 6, Ill.)

BOOK B RECORDS

PAGE	STORY	RECORD	TITLE
9	Wagon	CRG 1004	Little Red Wagon
29	Flat Sam	Columbia MJV 110	The Little Turtle (Burl Ives)
		LP	Yertle, the Turtle
		MSB 78010	Turtles, from Carnival of Animals, Saint-Saens
		CRG 1008	Castles in the Sand
		AED 22	Phoebe James Sea Life Rhythms
42	The Black Cow	CRG 5001	Ride 'Em Cowboy
		YPR 716	Little Cowboy
47	Black Mane and Tim	RCA E 71	Running Horses, Galloping Horses, High-Stepping Horses
51	Red Deer	RCA E 78	The Little Hunters
54	Seal	CRG 1028	I Am A Circus
65	Time for Bed	CRG 1024	Let's Be Firemen
		YPR 615	Little Firemen
74	The Lost Cow	YPR 716	The Little Cowboy
79	The Sad Goat		(See records for story on page 9)
83	Ride in a Jet Plane	YPR 706	Trains and Planes
		B Alb. B301	Rhythm Time (Mechanical Rhythms Record 1551)

Music Correlation for Basic Reading

Basic Music Series

Allyn and Bacon Co.	This is Music—2
American Book Company	American Singer 1 (2nd edition) American Singer 2 (2nd edition) Music for Young Americans 1 Music for Young Americans 2
Follett Publishing Co.	Together-We-Sing Series Music Round the Clock—1st Grade
Ginn and Company	Ginn, First Grade Ginn, Kindergarten
Silver Burdett Co.	Music for Early Childhood—Kindergarten Music Through the Day—1st Grade (Books of the Music for Living Series)

BOOK B SONG CORRELATION

PAGE	STORY TITLE	PAGE	SONG TITLE	MUSIC REFERENCE BOOK
2	The Cats and the Cart	90	Kitty	Music for Young Americans 1
		59	The Little Cat	Music for Early Childhood
		81	Cat and the Bird	American Singer 1 (2nd ed.)
		*23	I Love Little Pussy	Music Round the Clock
10	Pat and the Wagon	41	Little Red Wagon	Music Through the Day
		9	My Little Red Wagon	American Singer 1 (2nd ed.)
15	Ted and Rags	144	Oh Where, Oh Where	American Singer 1 (2nd ed.)
		143	Little Dog, What Do You Say?	Ginn, 1st Grade
		149	My Dog Jack	Ginn, 1st Grade
		*89	My Big Black Dog	Music for Young Americans 1
		77	Skipper	American Singer 1 (2nd ed.)
		*38	My Little Dog	Music Through the Day

* Denotes song is recorded in album that goes with series.

STORY PAGE	STORY TITLE	PAGE	SONG TITLE	MUSIC REFERENCE BOOK
29	Flat Sam	*68	Turtle	Music Through the Day
33	Balloons	*118	Little Day Moon	Ginn, 1st Grade
35	The Little Sled	36	Coasting	American Singer 1 (2nd ed.)
		37	Winter	American Singer 1 (2nd ed.)
42	The Black Cow	*55	Feeding Time	Music Through the Day
		153	Bossy Cow	Ginn, 1st Grade
47	Black Mane and Tim	149	Trot, Trot, Trot	Ginn, 1st Grade
51	Red Deer	42	A-Hunting We Will Go	Ginn, Kindergarten
54	Seal	*115	The Seal	Ginn, 1st Grade
60	The Milk Maid and Her Pail	82	Jack and Jill	Ginn, 1st Grade
65	Time for Bed	92	Playing Firemen	Music Through the Day
74	The Lost Cow	*61	Leading the Cows	Music Through the Day
		75	The Cowboy	Music for Young Americans 2
		37	Happy Cowboy	Music for Young Americans 1
		56	My Dream	Ginn, Kindergarten
79	The Sad Goat	77	The Hungry Goat	Music for Young Americans 1
		130	Mister Ramgoat	This is Music, 2
69	Ride in a Jet Plane	134	Airplane	Ginn, Kindergarten
		134	I'm an Airplane	Ginn, Kindergarten
		180	Aeroplane	Ginn, 1st Grade
		36	Jet Planes	Music for Young Americans 2

FILMSTRIP CORRELATIONS

Index of sources:

Cur: Curriculum Films
EBF: Encyclopaedia Britannica Films
Eye Gate: Eye Gate House
FOM: Popular Science Publishing Company
Jam Handy: The Jam Handy Organization
McG: McGraw-Hill Films
SVE: Society for Visual Education

OUR STORY	PAGE	FILMSTRIP TITLE	SOURCE
The Cats and the Cart	2	My Cat Taffy	Eye Gate
Ted and Rags	15	Paul's Puppy	EBF
		The Puppy	McG
The Cow and the Frog	24	The Biggest Frog in the World	Cur
		The Rabbits and the Frogs	McG
Flat Sam	29	The Turtles	Cur
		Terry's Turtle	EBF
		The Rabbit and the Turtle	Eye Gate
		My Turtle	Eye Gate
		The Turtle	McG
		Tubby Turtle	SVE
The Little Sled	35	Winter is Here	SVE
		Winter Adventures	SVE
The Black Cow	42	Mr. Peet, Dairy Farmer	Cur
		Cows	Cur
		Cows on the Farm	Jam Handy
		The Story of Milk	SVE
Black Mane and Tim	47	Horses on the Farm	Jam Handy
		Hoppy, the Rabbit	Jam Handy
Red Deer	51	The Deer and the Haystack	SVE
Don and Nell Dig Clams	55	Low Tide at the Beach	Cur
		To the Seashore	Eye Gate
		Animals of Sea and Shore	SVE
		Oceans	SVE
		Finding Out About Things Around Us	SVE
		A Visit to the Seashore	EBF

OUR STORY	PAGE	FILMSTRIP TITLE	SOURCE
Time for Bed	65	Firemen at Work	Cur
		The Fireman	Jam Handy
		The Story of Fire	FOM
		The Fireman	McG
The Lost Cow	74	To a Farm	Eye Gate
		Tom's Farm House	Eye Gate
		Cowboys	SVE
The Sad Goat	79	Three Billy Goats Gruff	Cur
		The Goat Farm	Cur
		The Three Billy Goats Gruff	Jam Handy
		Billy the Goat	Eye Gate
		The Boy and His Goats	McG
		The Goat That Went to School	SVE
Ride in a Jet Plane	83	Airplanes at Work	Cur
		To an Airport	Eye Gate
		The Airplane Does Many Jobs	FOM
		Airports and Airplanes	SVE
		What Makes an Airplane Fly?	Jam Handy
		How Is an Airplane Controlled?	Jam Handy
		How Do Jets Fly?	Jam Handy
		Rocket Power for Space Travel	Jam Handy
		Airplanes	Jam Handy
		Safety in Flight	Jam Handy
		How Do Helicopters Fly?	Jam Handy

MOTION PICTURE CORRELATIONS

Index of sources:
Coronet: Coronet Films
EBF: Encyclopaedia Britannica Films
McG: McGraw-Hill Films

OUR STORY	PAGE	FILM TITLE	SOURCE
The Cats and the Cart	2	Three Little Kittens	EBF
		Kitty Cleans Up	McG
		Mittens, the Kitten	Coronet
Ted and Rags	15	Shep, the Farm Dog	EBF
		Tippy, the Town Dog	EBF
		Frank and His Dog	EBF
		Our Pet Show	Coronet
		Peppy, the Puppy	Coronet
		Adventuring Pups	McG
The Cow and the Frog	24	The Cow and the Sprite	Coronet
		Tad, the Frog	Coronet
		The Frog Princess	Coronet
Flat Sam	29	Hare and the Tortoise	EBF
		Tuffy, the Turtle	Coronet
		The Toad and the Turtle Race	McG
The Little Sled	35	Play in the Snow	EBF
		Children in Winter	EBF
		Winter on the Farm	EBF
The Black Cow	42	Judy Learns About Milk	McG
		Frisky, the Calf	Coronet
Black Mane and Tim	47	Pride, the Saddle Horse	EBF
		Adventures of Bunny Rabbit	EBF
		Hoppy, the Bunny	Coronet
		Sparky, the Colt	Coronet
Red Deer	51	Spotty, Story of a Fawn	Coronet
		Spotty, the Fawn in Winter	Coronet
		Mother Deer and Her Twins	EBF
Don and Nell Dig Clams	55	We Visit the Seashore	McG
		We Explore the Beach	Coronet
		Sea Adventures of Sandy, the Snail	EBF

OUR STORY	PAGE	FILM TITLE	SOURCE
Time for Bed	65	The Fireman	EBF
		The Helpful Little Fireman	Coronet
		City Fire Fighters	Coronet
The Lost Cow	74	The Dairy Farm	Coronet
		A Visit with Cowboys	EBF
The Sad Goat	79	Billy and Nanny (The Twin Goats)	EBF
		Adventures of Two Little Goats	Coronet
Ride in a Jet Plane	83	Fred and Billy Take an Airplane Trip	Coronet
		The Busy Airport	Coronet
		Billy's Helicopter Ride	Coronet
		Airport in the Jet Age	EBF
		An Airplane Trip by Jet	EBF
		Our Shrinking World	EBF
Van's Cave	88	The Ugly Duckling	EBF

Acknowledgments

Editorial Assistance by Carolyn Shoaff, New Castle, Pennsylvania.
Music Enrichment Materials by Anita E. Scott, New Castle Area Schools, Pennsylvania.
Illustrations by Carol Kitzmiller and Ann Atene.

GLENN McCRACKEN
NEW CASTLE AREA SCHOOLS
NEW CASTLE, PENNSYLVANIA

CHARLES C. WALCUTT
QUEENS COLLEGE
FLUSHING, NEW YORK

B
BOOK

LIPPINCOTT'S BASIC READING

J. B. LIPPINCOTT COMPANY
PHILADELPHIA
NEW YORK

STANDARD BOOK NUMBER ISBN-397-43308-5
25.7210.9

CONTENTS

ar

arm darn tar dart tart cart

art card mar hard harm part

are star car farm far scarf

The Cats and the Cart

Tom is a farm hand.
Tom has a farm cart.

A card is on the cart.
Tom puts eggs in his cart.

Tom runs off to get a tart.
Tom is far from the cart.

The cats are at the cart.

Can the cats harm the eggs?

The cats harm the eggs.

And the eggs harm the cats.

er

fast faster
tend tender
damp damper
farm farmer
her

start starter
hunt hunter
camp camper
mend mender

ed

hand	handed	mend	mended
start	started	hunt	hunted
dent	dented	dart	darted

upon	under	forest	tennis	pepper
into				garden

ed

farm	farmed	camp	camped
harm	harmed	darn	darned

ed

cross	crossed	muss	mussed
stamp	stamped	miss	missed
gasp	gasped	mess	messed

w W

wet went west wig wag
win were winter western wagon
want wasp was water

Pat and the Wagon

Winter had wet the grass.
Sam darted into the garden.

Win started to run to him.
And Wag went fast to Win.

Pat, the cat, sat on the wagon.
The wagon had run into wet sand.

Wet sand is not hard.
The wagon dug into it fast.

Sam got to the wagon.
And Win and Wag were at the spot.

Pat got as sad as a winter sun.
And the wagon crept in faster.

Sam and Win and Wag dug in.
The wagon started up.

Pat got on the wagon.
Pat got into the garden.

w W

war wart warm swarm

Ted and Rags

Rags ran into the water.
The water was warm.

Ted wanted to run in the water.
Ted did not want to get wet.
Rags got wetter and wetter.

"Get it, Rags, get it," said Ted.
"Get the gun in the water."

Rags went to get the gun.
Rags got wetter and wetter.

said

Rags got the gun for Ted.
Ted went to Rags to get it.

Rags was wet.
Rags got the water off.

The water went from him to Ted.
The water was on Ted.

"The water is wet," said Ted.
"The water is wet and warm."

w W

saw	paw	raw	caw
draw	dawn	fawn	

A Fawn at Dawn

Sam handed Win a gun.
Win handed Sam a dart.

Sam and Win went into the forest.
Fawns were in the forest.

At dawn, Win saw a fat fawn.
The fawn saw Sam and Win.

It started to run fast.
It ran under a winter camp tent.

Sam and Win hunted for the fawn.
It hid in the tent.

Sam started to the farm.
Sam must not harm a fawn.

Win and Sam went to the farm.
Win wanted to get warm.

The raw winter dug into his hands.
Win and Sam did not harm the fawn.

ow

how now cow down town

The Cow and the Frog

A fat frog sat on a raft.
A tan cow saw the fat frog.
The cow sat down on the raft.

Down, down went the raft.
It went down into the water.

Now the cow sits in the water.
The frog sits on the cow.

l L

lag	lad	log	lap	let	leg
lip	last	less	lint	list	lost

clan	class	clap	clod	clam	slip
slat	slap	slit	slop	slam	glad
flat	flag	flip	flop	plot	plug
plan	plant	canal	helmet		

ll

all	tall	fall	call	hall	stall
wall	well	will	hill	till	still
mill	pill	sill	small		
pull	full	pullet			

Pull the full pan.

Put the water in the pot.

Ellen on a hill-top
Ellen on a hill
Ellen on a hill-top-hill
Still, still, still

Adele H. Seronde

Flat Sam

Ten small clams sat in the sand.
The clams sat under a log.
The water was still and warm.

Clams can dig in the sand.

The clams saw Flat Sam.
Flat Sam wanted to get the clams.

A clam called,
"Dig, clams, dig!
Get under the sand!
Dig far into the sand!"

Flat Sam swam after the clams.
The clams dug and dug in the sand.
Will Flat Sam get the clams?

Flat Sam swam fast to the log.

Slap, slap went the water.
Flat Sam did not get the clams.

The small clams were in the sand.
The small clams had dug far down.

b B

ban	bat	bar	bad	Ben	best
bed	beg	bin	bid	big	bond

but	bug	rob	rub	rib	tub
cob	cub	hub	stab	stub	bog
bit	bled	blimp	blot	barn	belt

dab	bib	brim	crab	slab	bass
bet	bag	bald	bump	brag	bulb
bull	bun	cab	ball	Bob	bend

le

bottle little apple rattle

The Little Sled

Bob and Ben sat on a little sled.
The sled started to run fast.
It ran down the big hill.

Faster and faster went the sled.
Bob and Ben held on to it.
"Stop the sled!" said Bob.

The sled hit a bump.
Bob and Ben fell from the sled.

The little sled did not stop.
It ran on and on.
It ran into a red barn.

The barn bent the little sled.
And the sled dented the barn.

Bob and Ben got wet.

k K

kit kill kept kiss kid keg
milk silk task mask risk brisk
kin dark lark park bark mark
ask kilt kitten

Mitten, mitten
  A mitten on a cat.
Kitten, kitten
  A kitten on a mat.

Adele H. Seronde

ck

rack	sack	tack	pack	lack	back
neck	deck	peck	nick	sick	tick
pick	wick	lick	mock	rock	sock

dock	lock	tuck	luck	buck	stack
stick	stock	stuck	pluck	smack	snack
black	track	truck	trick	flock	kick

A camel had an Arab on his back.
A camel had an Arab on his back.
The Arab sat
upon his hump—
Bump, bump, bump.
A camel had an Arab on his back.

Adele H. Seronde

nk

rank	tank	sink	ink	pink
sank	bank	drink	rink	mink
Frank	drank	sunk	link	wink

The Black Cow

Bob has a black cow.
The cow is kept in a barn.
Bob rubs her back and neck.
The cow will not harm Bob.

Bob wants to get milk.
Bob can milk his black cow.

Tab is a tan cat.
The cat begs for a drink of milk.
Bob milks the cow for Tab.

a A

can	cane	mat	mate
at	ate	fat	fate
rat	rate	man	mane
cap	cape	pan	pane

a A

car	care	bar	bare
mar	mare	star	stare
par	pare	far	fare
dare	hare	ware	flare

a A

name late Kate safe base bake
tale date blame make sake lake
taste same came slate fade male

gale bale stale take sale hate
gate state grate game pale mane
tame skate rake

Black Mane and Tim

Black Mane was a pet mare.
Her mane was black as slate.

Tim was a small, brown hare.

Black Mane and Tim ate grass.

Tim saw a snake in the grass.
The snake came up to Tim.
Tim saw the snake stare at him.
It was a big, black snake.

Black Mane ran to the gate.
Tim was on her back.
Tim made Black Mane run fast.
"Run, Black Mane, run!" said Tim.

Black Mane came to the gate.
It was as tall as the mare.
"Help, Tim!" said Black Mane.

Tim helped Black Mane.
Black Mane helped Tim.
The snake did not get the hare.

e E

ee

he	be	we	Pete	here

bee	see	seem	seed	seek	steel
flee	beet	beef	meet	deer	reel
deep	keep	peek	peel	feel	tree

feed	feet	need	steep	week	keen
deeper	feeler	keeper	fifteen	steed	

been

Red Deer

Red Deer went to a beet farm.
He wanted to feed on the beets.
The deer did not see the farmer.
The farmer did not want Red Deer to nip the tops off his beets.
The beet farmer hid under a tree.
He had a stick.

The farmer picked up the stick
and started after Red Deer.

Red Deer ran down a steep hill.
He hid in the deep grass.
But the farmer saw his antlers.

Red Deer swam
across the deep water.

He ran into the tall trees.

The farmer did not hit him.

Red Deer will not be back
to the beet farm.

He will not nip the tops
off the beets.

He will feed in the forest and
be safe from the farmer.

ea

ear bean leak meat reap neat
eat fear lean pea seam read

east feast leap peak seat near
ease heat lease tea bead beak
beat heal least seal team please

beam leaf meal rear tease beard
beast lead mean sea dear pleat
repeat retreat steam defeat

Don and Nell Dig Clams

Don and Nell went to the sea to dig clams.

Nell wanted clams to eat.

Don had a bucket and a rake on the end of a stick.

He and Nell dug for clams.

"We will steam the clams," said Don.

"I will heat the water," said Nell.

Don and Nell steamed the bucket of clams.

I

"Please pass me a clam," said Nell.

Nell ate ten clams for her meal. Don ate fifteen clams.

After the big meal, Don and Nell were full of clams.

ai

aim	raise	rain	waist	hair	grain
air	gain	main	lair	maid	braid
faint	fail	bail	rail	hail	mail
paid	tail	claim	drain	brain	train

sail pain Spain gait slain stain
plain pail nail bait wait trailer
again sprain praise strain paint
sailor

An ant
Will pass
In a forest
Of grass
On a twig
Near a rain-
Puddle
Sea.
And a rock
Will be
A hill
Tip-top
And a fern
A monster
Tree.

Adele H. Seronde

The Milk Maid and Her Pail

A milk maid named Gail went to market.

Gail had her pail of milk on top of her braided hair.

The milk maid skipped and began to plan.

"I will trade the milk for a hen at the market," said Gail.

"I will get eggs from the hen, and I will sell the eggs."

"After I sell the eggs, I will get a silk dress.

"I need a silk dress to make all the lads at the market run up and speak to me.

"And I will toss my braids in the air."

my

Gail tossed her braids back.

The pail fell off and all the milk was spilled.

The sad milk maid did not get a hen, or eggs, or a silk dress.

or

i I

ie

mine ride pile swine bite spike
pine side pike tile dime strike
nine hide time like pipe spite

fine wide life stile smile bride
line ripe mile lime stride diner
kite wife spine dike crime finer

find kind mind bind grind behind

tie lie die pie cried dried tried

ir

sir	fir	firm	bird	girl	dirt
sire	fire	spire	hire	tire	first

Time for Bed

It is time for Bill and Mike to be in bed.

"I like to be in bed at nine," said Bill.

"I will be in bed first."

Mike snapped off the lamp.

Mike and Bill had a fine bed in a tent.

It was a big, wide bed.

It was raised on a pair of blocks.

"I see a man," cried Bill.

"He has dark hair. Hide under the blanket. I am afraid."

Mike and Bill hid under the red and black blanket.

"Lie still," said Mike.

"The man cannot see us. Do not be scared."

The man saw Mike and Bill.

Mike peeked at him.

do

"Wake up, Mike," cried the man.

"The tent is on fire."

Mike and Bill ran from the tent. Bill saw the man first. It was Farmer Tom.

He had a spade with him.

He dug and tossed dirt on the fire.

"Farmer Tom is a fine man," said Bill.

"He came in time to stop the fire."

go no so

hole mole sole lone pole home
bone cone alone stone rode robe
smoke globe hope note poke stole
rose rope dose dome lope nose
tone drone

post most colt bolt host
holster poster old hold told

come some done

ore or

ore	more	core	pore	wore
fore	lore	sore	bore	shore
before	horse	tore		

or	for	nor	fork	corn
horn	born	torn	worn	cord
cork	lord	ford		

A little elf
Sat by himself
   Alone,
Alone in the lap
Of an acorn cap
   At home.

Adele H. Seronde

The Lost Cow

Ted Lane rode his horse into the hills.

He went to find a lost cow.

Ted wore a gun.

He had taken his braided rope from its nail near the corral. He had put the rope on his saddle.

He wanted to rope the lost cow and take her back home.

Ted came to a water hole.

He saw some tracks his cow had made in the mud.

"I hope the lost cow is near," said Ted. "I want to find her before dark."

Ted saw more and more tracks in the sand and in the wet grass.

"Now I will find the cow," said Ted. "Her tracks go here."

Ted rode to the top of a big hill.

He saw a man and a cow.

"The man stole my cow," said Ted. "I will take her from him."

Ted started down the big hill.

He had his rope in his hand.

"Stop!" Ted cried.

The man did not stop.

Ted spun his rope in the air and made it sail at the man.

"I hope I can rope the man and the cow," he said.

Ted got the cow in his rope.

"Now I can take the cow home," said Ted. "The bad man will not get her."

oa

oat roam cloak board boat goal

oak loaf soap hoarse soar moan

oar road coat coarse roar groan

goat toad croak soak foam coal

oe

toe foe hoe woe goes

does

The Sad Goat

Once upon a time a goat sat near the side of a road. He was an old, fat goat. His coat was black as coal.

The goat saw a green toad go down the road. "I want to hop like a toad," said the fat old goat. "I want to hop, hop, hop down the road."

once

"A fat goat cannot hop," said the oak tree. "A frog can hop like a toad, but a fat goat cannot hop at all."

"I can hop if I want to," said the goat. "I will leap into the road now."

The old goat made a big leap for a fat goat. But he did not land on the road.

"Help me!" said the goat. "Help me get down from here! I cannot hop like a toad! I hop like a fat goat."

"The goat will not boast now," said the tall oak tree. "He will not boast how far he can leap."

j J

jet	jig	jar	jag
job	Jeff	jog	jam
just	jug	James	jerk

jump	Jess	jaw	jot
Jack	Jim	Jones	joke
Jill	Jean	jab	junk
Jan	jeep	jail	Joan

Ride in a Jet Plane

Jack went on a trip in a jet plane. It was his first plane ride. He went to see Jan. Jan's home was in West Falls.

A jet plane is big and it can go fast. It is as sleek as a bird. Jack had not seen a plane as big as the Star Fire.

The big plane sat still and Jack went up the steps.

Jack sat down near the back of the plane. He had a seat belt to make him safe.

Jack saw the pilot in the front of the plane. His job was to run the Star Fire. Jack saw the hostess. Her job was to help Jack if he sent for her. The hostess was to get him a meal if it was time to eat.

"I press a little button if I want to eat," said Jack.

Jack ate on the big plane. He had meat and rolls and jam.

"Just like home!" said Jack. "I can eat, and read, and sleep if I want to."

The Star Fire came to West Falls on time. Jack ran down the steps.

Jan came in a jeep to meet Jack and take him home.

"I had fun on the big jet plane," Jack told Jan.

v V

van	stove	five	save
vent	alive	wave	over
vest	dive	wove	Rover
vile	gave	leave	diver
vote	pave	weave	vacant
volt	cave	cove	silver
vow	hive	eave	sliver

live	give	love	move
liver	have	glove	dove

Van's Cave

Van is an old, old man. He lives in a cave near a lake. Van has a bed and a stove in the cave.

Van made the bed of old lumber. He made the stove of old bricks. He sleeps in the bed. Spot likes to sleep near the stove. His bed is just an old coat.

Spot likes to live in Van's cave. It is home for the old man and the dog.